FLY FISHING
FOR BASS

FLY FISHING FOR BASS

Smallmouth, Largemouth, Exotics

LEFTY KREH

THE LYONS PRESS
Guilford, Connecticut
An imprint of The Globe Pequot Press

The Lyons Press is an imprint of The Globe Pequot Press.

10 9 8 7 6 5 4 3 2 1

Printed in the United States of America

ISBN 1-59228-310-1

Frontispiece: *The Potomac River, in Washington, D.C., is a great largemouth spot.*

Cover photograph of popping bugs by Dave Whitlock.

Color photography by :
        Andy Anderson (page 72)
        Cathy and Barry Beck (pages 17, 32)
        Lefty Kreh (pages 2, 21, 22, 24, 29, 65, 92/93, 106/107, 120)
        Dave Whitlock (page 13)

Illustrated by Rod Walinchus, Livingston, Montana.

Library of Congress Cataloging-in-Publication Data is available on file.

CONTENTS

INTRODUCTION 7

A BRIEF NATURAL HISTORY OF THE MAJOR
SPECIES OF BASS 13

   Largemouth Bass 13

   Smallmouth Bass 17

   The Exotics 21

      Peacock Bass 21

      Niugini and Spottailed Bass 22

THE DIFFERENCES BETWEEN SMALL AND
LARGEMOUTH BASS FROM AN ANGLER'S
PERSPECTIVE 25

TACKLE FOR BASS 33

   Rods 33

   Reels 34

   Lines 35

      Sink-Tip Line Applications 36

      Full-Sinking Line Applications 38

      Shooting Head Applications 38

   Leaders 39

Flies 41
  Smallmouth Bass Flies 41
  Largemouth Bass Flies 49

Some General Observations about the Selection
of Bass Flies 62

FLY FISHING FOR BASS IN RIVERS, LAKES, SMALL
STREAMS AND PONDS 73

  Introductory Note 73

  Watersheds for Bass 74
    Large Rivers 74
    Small Streams 88
    Lakes 91
    Farm Ponds 94

  The Seasons of the Bass 98
    Summer 98
    Late Spring/Early Fall 103
    Cold Weather 104

  Special Retrieving Techniques for Bass 113

  Night Fishing for Smallmouths 116

THE EXOTICS 121

  Peacock Bass 121

  Niugini and Spottailed Bass 130

INDEX 140

INTRODUCTION

It might surprise many fly fishermen, but the most popular sport fish in the United States is the bass, both large and smallmouth. There are some states that have no trout, or very few. But *every state* has bass. While I know there are some snobbish trout fishermen who believe that trout are so much more difficult to catch on a fly than a bass, that's simply not true. You may think that a wise old brown trout sipping minuscule midges off a slick surface is a tough adversary, but wait until you try to catch a largemouth bass from the gin-clear waters of a limestone quarry! It took several years for me to solve the mystery of how to catch one of these bass. And to successfully take smallmouth bass from lakes is a challenge worthy of any fly fisherman. If you are looking for a fish that is difficult to deceive on a fly rod, look no further, for all species of bass will fit the bill.

A fish biologist once pointed out to me that two of the best built predator fish were the saltwater grouper and the bass, two species constructed along the same efficient lines. Bass have a relatively short body, which allows them to chase their prey and turn corners sharply while pursuing it. Contrast that capability to a fish anglers generally regard as a superb predator, the barracuda. While the barracuda is capable of attaining breathtaking speeds, its long body doesn't allow it to turn sharply if the prey darts to the side. Also, the broad tail of the bass permits it to achieve great acceleration from a dead stop, making it a near-perfect ambush predator. And, the big mouth of all species of bass (for despite its name, even the smallmouth is equipped with a sizeable mouth) makes it easy for bass to engulf prey.

Bass can be found in a wide variety of watersheds: warm or cold water lakes; big, brawling rivers; the lower ends of mountain streams; tidal creeks and rivers; limestone rivers; small creeks; farm ponds; tanks; and a host of other places. If there is relatively pure water that is not too cold, there are probably bass there.

We commonly think of large and smallmouth bass as being North American fish, but bass can be found in other parts of the world, too. I was once lucky enough to fish Treasure Lake, in Zapata Swamp in Cuba, in 1959. Using popping bugs and hackle streamers, we caught a number of largemouth bass that exceeded 10 pounds. It was the best trophy largemouth bass fishery I have ever encountered. But, I have also had fun on bass in Mexico, as well as many other Central American countries.

There are a number of subspecies of the sunfish family (Centrarchidae) of which black bass are members, but this book will be dealing principally with our two most sporting subspecies, the largemouth and the smallmouth. (Though, I have added a short description at the end of the book of the exotic basslike species that are now becoming popular with the traveling angler.) And since the large and smallmouth bass are close cousins of each other, it probably won't come as a big surprise that these two species are fished for in essentially the same way, with the same tackle and techniques.

*****

I can clearly remember catching my first bass on a fly rod. I was 21 years old in 1947. Freshly returned from World War II and unmarried, I became a fly-fishing fool. Near my home in central Maryland was a small, clear stream that ran through a lush pasture. One day, as I was prowling the banks armed with my new fly rod, I saw several 12 to 14-inch bass in a 40-foot-long pool. Creeping closer along the bank, I got into position and made a rather clumsy cast of a popping bug upstream of the fish. Then I twitched the popper several times as it drifted down to the bass. Two of the fish moved upward slightly, looked at the popper, and then dropped back to resume their holding positions in the current. After several failures with this technique, I put on a marabou streamer that the tackle store recommended. The fish ignored it, too.

That began my first lesson in fly fishing for bass, which is to watch and learn. I lay on the bank of the stream and spent the next 20 minutes just observing what these bass were doing. One chased a minnow, while the others held in the current. After I had intently watched these fish for perhaps five minutes, I saw one surge to the surface, grab something and drop below. This was repeated a few minutes later by another nearby bass. I switched my concentration from the bass to the surface. A few minutes later I saw a "wrinkle" in the surface as a struggling grasshopper, blown to the water by the summer breeze, came drifting along. A bass rose and took the hopper. This happened several times during the long period that I observed these fish. My head was spinning. I lay there wondering what I could do. I didn't want to put a grasshopper on a bare hook — I *really* wanted to catch one of these bass on a fly!

Finally, I came up with an idea, although I didn't know if it would work. The popping bug I had on my leader was typical of those of that period: a painted cork on a hook, dressed with rubber bands. It had a tail of hackles splayed and extending well behind the hook, and a half-inch of feathers spiraled between the tail and the bug body. I pulled the rubber bands from the bug body. And then I trimmed away most of the spiraled hackle and cut the tail feathers with a knife so that they extended only a short distance behind the bug body. I hated to deface a nice bug like that, but I wanted to try something different.

Now that I had my fly dressed the way I wanted it, I crept away from the river out into the meadow and caught perhaps two dozen grasshoppers. Crawling back to the bank, upstream from the fish, I dropped a live hopper on the water. It floated downstream and disappeared into the mouth of one of the bass. Smiling, I began to toss more hoppers in the stream. It was fun to watch, as I saw three bass competing to see which could get to the hoppers first. After I had used most of the hoppers I had collected, I crawled just downstream from the feeding bass and simultaneously threw three hoppers upstream from the bass, and then cast my mangled popping bug alongside the struggling live hoppers, twitching my line to give the popping bug an imitation of natural action. As the live hoppers came into range, all three smallmouths rose to grab them. But one bass was so anxious that instead of taking a live hopper it grabbed my popping bug. I was so astonished that I didn't even set the hook. But the bass was so greedy it did the job for me, and I was fast to my first bass on a fly rod.

Few fish I have caught in my long career have ever pleased me so much. That was 47 years ago, and I remember it like it was yesterday. I was ecstatic. After landing it I shouted with glee! I couldn't believe how hard my heart was pumping. I confess that I brought that 14-inch smallmouth home to show my friends. This was also my first lesson in chumming or teasing fish.

While people have been fly fishing for bass for a long time, I suppose, when I started in earnest in the late 1940s there was almost no one in my region of the country who was bass fishing with a fly rod. Certainly few people knew little more than to use a popping bug or a simple streamer, and to make a short cast that would result in a shorter retrieve, a pick-up and another cast.

I recall that when I really got into the sport in the late 1940s, I would take only my fly rod and fish mainly on the Potomac River in Maryland, although I sampled many rivers in Virginia and Pennsylvania, too. In those days I was trying to convince myself and others that I could catch bass. So, I would bring back full stringers of dead fish. Frequently I would have a daily limit (10 bass) on a stringer, including some very nice three to four-pound smallmouths.

In those days, it was rare for the average fisherman to ever catch his limit of smallmouth, although the local rivers were full of fish. So when I brought my stringers into the boat docks, people would ask me what I caught the fish on. I would explain I caught them on a fly rod. They wouldn't believe me. So then I would show them that all I had in my boat were some popping bugs, simple streamers, a fly rod, a line, and a reel. Several times I heard someone mumble that I had actually used bait on my fly-fishing tackle — or else was keeping something secret from them.

Also back then, there was no one I could get advice from, and so I began the painful experience of learning to fly fish on my own. At that time, the traditional and recommended casting method was to move the fly rod from nine o'clock to one o'clock, and then return it back to nine o'clock. But gradually, I began to realize that the longer you moved the rod through the casting arc, the easier all casting became. And so it was in those early days, bass fishing for hours at a time, attempting to throw the longest line I could, that I began to develop the casting method that I teach today.

Fortunately, things have changed greatly since I began fly fishing. We now have superb fly rods, wonderful light reels, and an array of specialized fly lines that can be matched to specific fishing situations. Many thousands of fly fishermen — maybe even hundreds of thousands — now avidly seek bass, and there are numerous magazine articles, books, videos, seminars and clubs devoted to fly fishing for bass.

You will find there are many parallels between angling for the bass and the trout on a fly rod. For example, each species can be caught at night on flies — and these are frequently the trophy fish. In fact, I've found that night fishing was the ticket to catching quarry bass. Also, just as over a long period of years we have created a body of literature about how to achieve success in fly fishing for trout, fly fishing for bass has in modern times developed its own set of special techniques and tactics. Of course, that's what this book is about. If you are already a dedicated bass fly fisherman, I hope the book will assist you in catching more and bigger bass — and have more fun doing it. And if you've never tried it before, I hope what I have to say will get you interested in bass fishing with a fly rod, as it is a superb angling experience.

A BRIEF NATURAL HISTORY OF THE MAJOR SPECIES OF BASS

By Harry Middleton

LARGEMOUTH BASS

Largemouth bass. Micropterus salmoides. One of the most popular and important gamefish in the world, a fish greatly admired and much sought after by legions of anglers, including fly fishermen. Like most bass, the largemouth carries an interesting array of names. In some waters of North America it is called the green bass; in others it is known as the black bass. No matter its local monikers, the many names anglers heaped upon it, the largemouth's great bucket-shaped mouth, its size and strength, its tenacity distinguish it among bass, among all freshwater gamefish.

The largemouth is the largest member of the sunfish family. Sunfish, which number at least thirty species, are indigenous to North America. One of the six species of so-called black bass, it is easy to distinguish the largemouth bass from all its close cousins, including the smallmouth bass. The word "bass" is thought to come from the old English word *baers*, meaning bristles or thorny. And, indeed, the dorsal fin of bass has a distinctive thorny feel to it. Too, the dorsal fin of the largemouth is not continuous — as it is on the smallmouth — and its base is not marked by covering scales, as is that of the smallmouth. And as their popular names imply, another anatomical difference between these two members of the family bass is the larger mouth of the largemouth, which is distinguished by an upper jaw that extends well behind its eyes.

Perhaps the most obvious difference between the fish, however, is their coloring. Because of their warm golden color, smallmouth bass are often called bronzebacks. Sunlight flashing off the iridescent back of a smallmouth bass glows the color of polished bronze or, in low light, the color of melted honey, a tapestry of soft golden browns. By contrast, the largemouth's colors are much darker, burnt greens, with an unmistakable black, often thick, horizontal stripe running along the entire length of its flanks. Among large, adult largemouth bass, this dark stripe is often all but invisible, blending perfectly with the fish's deep green coloring.

Certainly among the world's most adaptable and prolific members of the bass family, in North America largemouths are found in nearly every state. These handsome fish, marked by their great homocercal tails and heavy, thick flanks, are known for their ferocity more than their cunning or grace. They are slow and have a total distaste for moving water. Their passion is for stillwater.

Originally, the home waters of the largemouth bass reached from the waters of southeastern Canada south into the Great Lakes and then down into the warmer climes of the Mississippi River Valley, then on southward through the Deep South and into Mexico. To the east, largemouth bass are also part of the indigenous fish populations that came to thrive in freshwater lakes and rivers from Maryland down the Atlantic coast to the warm, fecund waters of Florida, which provide what is perhaps the ultimate largemouth bass habitat.

Largemouth bass have proved incredibly tenacious fish and have been successfully introduced to a variety of freshwater habitats throughout North and South America, including the colder waters of New England and some of the rivers of the Northwest, such as the sprawling Columbia River drainage.

While largemouth bass can survive and thrive in a wide variety of water conditions, they prefer warm, shallow lakes and rivers. The weedier or grassier the aquatic habitat, the better the largemouth like it. Such heavy grassbeds provide both excellent cover and important hunting grounds for largemouths. It is rare to find significant concentrations of largemouth bass in deep water (down below 15 to 20 feet) or in water that is not marked by substantial stands of aquatic vegetation.

Largemouth bass spawn in the spring in warming water. Before active spawning can begin, the water temperature must be a constant 60 to 65 degrees. In the southern reaches of their range, largemouths will begin spawning as early as late April or early May, while farther to the north the water may not be warm enough for spawning until well into June or early July.

When spawning, the male bass will prepare the nest, using its body to scrape out a small depression in the bottom. The average nest is about five inches deep and about 20 inches in diameter. Largemouth bass usually like to spawn as close to cover (either the shoreline or among the grassbeds) as possible and in fairly shallow water. Largemouths are solitary, aggressive and territorial, even in spawning, and rarely will their nests be found close together. Once the nest is prepared and the female is satisfied with it, she will lay her eggs, several hundred at a time, which the male quickly fertilizes. Females spawn several times during the season, with several males. Consequently, several females usually end up laying eggs in each nest, so that the total number of eggs in each nest can number well into the thousands. Spawning females are egg-heavy, carrying anywhere from a thousand to eight thousand eggs for every pound of their body weight.

Among largemouth bass, it is the male, not the female, that guards the nest and eggs until they hatch, which happens within a week to ten days after fertilization. However, if the water temperature is well above 65 degrees — say between 75 and 80 degrees — the eggs will hatch more quickly.

Once the hatching fry have completely consumed their yolk sacs, they will begin to come off the nest, school, and keep close to shallow water and cover, feeding on plankton. Largemouth fry will school together until they have grown to at least an inch. At this stage, they are a pale sulfur yellow in color with an unmistakable black stripe running from tail to head. Tireless predators even at this size, by the time they have grown to two inches in length, the small largemouths are already feeding on small fish.

Largemouth bass are relatively long-lived fish. It is not uncommon for northern largemouth bass to live more than eight years. Growth is constant, so that by its second full year as an adult a northern largemouth bass will already average between nine and 12 inches in length. By the time it reaches full adulthood, say its seventh or eighth year, these northern largemouth bass can easily reach lengths of nearly 20 inches. Because of the presence of prey-rich water, water full of worms, frogs, insects and insect larvae, minnows, crayfish, on and on, and warm water nearly year round, southern largemouth bass, and especially the Florida largemouth bass, generally grow at a much faster rate. Too, these largemouth bass can grow to tremendous size. While a trophy-sized northern large-mouth bass might tip the scale at eight pounds, Florida largemouth bass of 12 pounds and more are occasionally landed. In warm southern waters, bass anglers dream of the largemouth bass that will go to 20 pounds. Large-mouths of such size have been caught in Georgia, South Carolina, and California.

SMALLMOUTH BASS

Among ichthyologists it is known as Micropterus dol-omieui. Among anglers it is simply the incomparable smallmouth bass, the glorious bronzeback. Many anglers, including a great many fly fishermen, firmly believe that the smallmouth bass is among the greatest freshwater gamefish found in North America, a black bass with the grace, fight, cunning, and intelligence of a trout.

Like their behemoth cousin, the largemouth bass, smallmouth bass are members of the sunfish family and are among the six species of black bass found in North American waters. The smallmouth is marked by its handsome bronze or warm brown coloring and the distinct, dark bars running vertically along its flanks. Young smallmouths are even more colorful, flashing a tricolored tail, the edges white and glowing orange, the center oil-black.

Too, the dorsal fin on the smallmouth is continuous, its line broken only by a small notch about halfway between the tail and head. In comparison to the bucket mouth of the largemouth bass, the mouth of the smallmouth is relatively small — which explains its name — never extending beyond the eyes. Even so, its mouth is sufficiently large to engulf surprisingly large minnows, frogs, and crayfish.

Like the largemouth bass, smallmouth bass have been successfully introduced throughout much of North America. Their range now extends from northeast Canada, south into Minnesota, then on into the warm waters of Maryland and Virginia, even as far south as northern Alabama. Too, the smallmouth's range includes some portions of the Midwest and west into parts of Kansas and eastern Oklahoma. Originally, smallmouth bass in North America were confined to a fairly small geographical range, being mainly found in the sprawling drainage systems of Lake Ontario to the north and south through the Ohio River drainage.

By the mid-1800s, however, anglers began trying to introduce the smallmouth bass to other waters. At first, smallmouth were introduced into the waters of the East, rather than the West. Smallmouth bass from the Ohio

River were released into the upper Potomac River. By the middle of this century, however, smallmouth bass had been introduced into a wide variety of watersheds from Canada to California, even though most of the great North American smallmouth bass water remains in the East — the Potomac, Shenandoah, Susquehanna, and James rivers.

Unlike their heavyweight cousins, smallmouth bass tend to do best in cooler water, in shallower lakes and in rivers. Perfect water for the smallmouth is that with a temperature range from 60 to 75 degrees. And again unlike the largemouth, they delight in moving water, in rivers and lakes marked by at least some current with rocky bottoms and water rich in food — smaller fish, a healthy population of insects and insect larvae, frogs and toads, and their favorite prey, crayfish.

Like most members of the bass family, smallmouth bass will mature at a rate that is dependent on the temperature and condition of their home waters. Usually, the warmer the water, the faster the rate of their maturation. Smallmouth bass living in colder northern waters might require as many as three full years to attain a length of seven to nine inches. In warmer southern waters, smallmouths will reach this same size, say nine inches, in two years, maybe fewer.

In spawning, smallmouth bass will use both large and small bodies of water, lakes and the mouths of streams, and smaller tributaries. Active spawning will not begin until the water temperature rises and stays above 65 degrees. In the southern limits of their range, rivers and lakes warm quickly and will reach this spawning temperature sometimes as early as April. And for the most part, generally by June or early July, most of the lakes and rivers holding smallmouths have warmed enough for spawning.

As with the largemouth, the male prepares the nest. Smallmouths will often dig their nests in deeper water. After a female has laid its eggs in the nest made by the male (it can be from 15 to 30 inches in diameter), it is quickly chased off, so that another female may be lured by the male to lay its eggs in the nest. It will take as many as three to four females to fill the nest with eggs. Female smallmouths generally carry from one thousand to six thousand eggs per pound of their body weight. The eggs will not hatch simultaneously. Depending on the number of eggs in a nest and the temperature of the water, incubation might require as little as a day or two, or more than a week. The hatched fry, which are coal black except for their golden eyes, evacuate the nest quickly, and are immediately on their own.

The smallmouth bass can be as long-lived as the largemouth. It continues to mature and grow throughout its life, so that a mature seven-year-old smallmouth bass will generally range, in size, from 16 to 20 inches.

There is no end to the good-natured quarreling among bass anglers over which is the better gamefish, largemouth or smallmouth.

Both are hailed, prized. Even so, when it comes to total cunning and sheer ferocity, especially for its size, there are very few freshwater gamefish that surpass the smallmouth bass and that includes the largemouth.

The fly fisherman skilled and lucky enough to take his first five-pound smallmouth will surely never forget the experience; he will place it among his most precious and most relived angling memories. Like so many trout, the smallmouth bass is another fish that, once hooked, is greater than the sum of its parts.

The active season for smallmouth is a long one, beginning in the spring in the southern regions of their range and extending well into the fall. Smallmouth bass are almost always most active during the early hours of the morning and the dwindling hours before twilight. These are the two times of day when you are most likely to find smallmouth bass feeding at the surface.

THE EXOTICS

PEACOCK BASS

There are many types of basslike species, the so-called exotic bass or jungle bass, scattered throughout the world. One of the most famous and most interesting, the peacock bass, is actually not a bass at all but a member of the freshwater cichlid fishes of the Cichlidae family, which are found in the waters of South America, parts of Africa, and southeastern Asia. In character and looks, the cichlids do indeed favor bass and the entire sunfish family. Smaller cichlids are extremely popular aquarium fish.

Among the larger cichlids, peacock bass have lately become popular gamefish. This challenging, fierce, and incredibly strong fish is found in large populations in the tropical rivers and lakes of South America. Known as *pavons* in South America, peacock bass resemble large-mouth bass, though on a far grander scale.

There are three species of peacock bass — the butterfly pavon (marked by three dark irregular spots along its lateral line and lovely blue-green and yellow coloring and a telltale bright eye); the royal or speckled pavon (the smallest of the pavons), a magnificently beautiful fish; and the peacock pavon, which is the largest of South America's peacock bass, marked by a series of nearly coal-black vertical stripes (from three to five) that appear on the fish's massive green to bronze-green flanks. These markings, plus the black spot found on the tail, along with their haunting black, red-lined eyes, make the peacock pavon a distinctive, unmistakable and unforgettable fish. It is this pavon's black spot from which it takes the name peacock, for it is very much like the silky black spot that decorates the male peacock's elaborate tail feathers.

The peacock pavon can reach great size. While these fish can indeed reach weights of up to 30 pounds, half that size, fish from 10 to 15 pounds, are far more common. The other species of peacock bass are somewhat smaller, with the royal pavon coming in mostly under 10 pounds and the butterfly pavon going as big as 10 pounds, especially in the tropical reaches of the Orinoco River.

NIUGINI AND SPOTTAILED BASS

As haunting as the pavon of South America are, there are even more exotic strains of bass found in even more remote corners of the world. Among exotic fish, perhaps none is more mysterious than the Niugini bass, which is found in the warm, tropical waters of New Guinea's rivers. Lying north of Australia, the island of New Guinea is actually divided into two distinct political states, the province of West Irian or Irian Jaya and Papua New Guinea, which is an independent nation. The island remains one of the wildest and most remote places left on the earth. Almost anything involving New Guinea, whether it is fishing its ancient waters or hiking its secluded jungles, remains a true adventure.

The Niugini bass is actually a black bass, a freshwater member of the Pacific black basses and a close relation of the spottailed bass. These aggressive and spectacular fish — which are also related to the cubera snapper that are found along the tropical coral reefs of the Caribbean and South America — are found throughout New Guinea's rivers. They are considered by the handful of sports fishermen that have challenged them to be among the fiercest and most powerful freshwater gamefish in the world. Though only a handful of fly fishermen have caught Niugini bass. In addition to being found in large numbers in many of New Guinea's rivers, both Niugini and spottailed bass can also be found just offshore of the island, especially in the waters off New Britain and the Arjjim islands.

OVERLEAF: *Les Adams with a smallmouth bass on the Penobscot River in Maine.*

CHAPTER ONE

THE DIFFERENCES BETWEEN SMALL AND LARGEMOUTH BASS FROM AN ANGLER'S PERSPECTIVE

After more than 50 years of catching both smallmouth and largemouth bass, I'm convinced that the smallmouth is a much better fighter than the largemouth. It jumps higher, runs faster and pulls longer against the rod. Even when caught in the same rivers or lakes, the smallmouth is a stronger adversary. That doesn't mean that I don't like largemouth bass — I do. But, so far as my experience is concerned, the smallmouth is the better fighting bass.

There are some visible differences in the two species, too. With its mouth closed, the largemouth has its jaw hinge to the rear or behind the eye; the smallmouth has the jaw hinge falling forward of the eye.

The smallmouth usually has vertical dark bars on its body from forward of the tail to just behind the gill cover. Such bars are often difficult to see, but in some cases are extremely noticeable. Largemouth bass do not have such

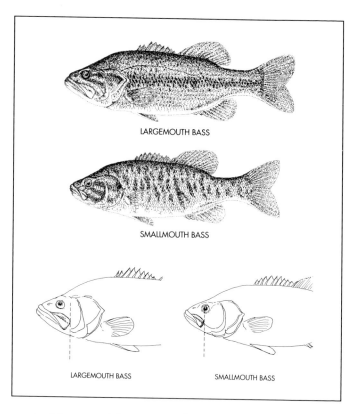

LARGEMOUTH BASS

SMALLMOUTH BASS

LARGEMOUTH BASS   SMALLMOUTH BASS

vertical bars, and have a much more pronounced lateral line (the sound receptor that runs from behind the gills to near the tail in the middle of each side of the body) that is very visible and usually well marked with dark lines. With smallmouths, the lateral line cannot be seen easily.

Smallmouth bass tend to be thinner for their length than do largemouths, although in some watersheds, especially lakes where there is a high abundance of food, the smallmouth can look almost like a football.

Smallmouth bass usually are found in waters with a slightly lower year-round temperature than largemouths.

I think that here is a place to make a point about bass and many other species that can be an important consideration concerning successful fly fishing.

I do not believe that fish are more "comfortable" in certain temperatures. Obviously, if the temperature nears freezing, or becomes excessively hot, then fish will be uncomfortable and may even die. But, what needs to be considered is that fish are not like humans so far as regulating their body temperature is concerned. If the air surrounding the human body is colder or hotter than normal body temperature, the body attempts to adjust things to retain the body's normal temperature. That's why we shiver when it's cold and sweat when it's hot. Fish have no such concerns. They accept the temperature of the water surrounding them. Thus, if the water is 58 degrees, the fish will also be that temperature. They do not try to regulate their body temperature to differ from the water they are immersed in.

But what is important is that the water temperature affects the metabolism of a fish. As water temperatures lower, so does the fish's body temperature. And its need for food and energy decreases. In effect, its engine runs slower. Thus, as water temperatures drop, the fish needs less food and energy, and so it moves around slower and feeds less. As temperatures rise, the fish's energy motor runs faster and demands more food and so the fish needs to eat more, but only up to a point. If temperatures get too high, the metabolism slows down again and so does the fish's body activities, so that again it requires less food.

What this means is that for all species of fish, when temperatures approach the lower or higher temperature limits *for that particular species*, the fish's feeding slows down. What is crucial then, in understanding fish behavior from the angler's perspective, and therefore what tactics and techniques to employ in response to a change in that behavior, is to know what are the lowest and highest temperatures affecting a species, *and at what temperatures does each species have the highest metabolic demands.*

Fortunately for bass anglers, scientists have determined this factor for the large and smallmouth bass. Smallmouth bass, especially those less than 12 inches long, will feed most actively when water temperatures range from 67 to 71 degrees. And in some warmer lakes, feeding activity may be pretty vigorous even if the temperature range is a little higher; the reason being that the water in lakes is colder a few feet deeper, and smallmouths will move up from this cooler sanctuary into the warmer waters just below the surface of the lake to grab their prey.

So here's a good rule to keep in mind: when fly fishing for smallmouth bass, the optimum conditions for success, that is, the time when the fish are feeding most vigorously, is when water temperatures are between 67 and 71 degrees.

In fact, in most watersheds, smallmouth bass less than 12 inches long seem to stop feeding altogether when water temperatures drop to about 50 degrees.

However, *big* smallmouths will continue to feed well into the fall and spring since they will put on a layer of fat when temperatures are between 55 and 40 degrees. So, in lakes and rivers, the spring and fall (again, when water temperatures are from 55 degrees down to as low as 40 degrees) are perhaps the most consistent times to have a real chance at catching a trophy smallmouth. Later in the book, I will discuss how to catch such bass during this period of the year.

The rule for largemouth: *The optimum water temperature range for largemouth bass is from about 67 to as high as 78 degrees.* However, in southern waters, where bass are

Early morning on a bass lake is a great time to fish. ➤

more consistently subjected to higher temperatures than elsewhere, *largemouths will frequently avidly feed into the low 80-degree range.*

I repeat, *understanding how metabolism affects the fish's feeding behavior is vital to fishing success.* I suggest that if you memorize the water temperatures given above to determine the optimum feeding conditions for either the small or largemouth species, you will probably have more fishing success when you are able to fish in water at those temperatures. But remember, bass are not *uncomfortable* if the water temperature is lower or higher, unless it gets excessively hot or cold.

Let me give just one example of how understanding this temperature concept can improve your fishing. If you fish a river in the central or northern part of the United States in summer, for example, where the water temperatures may be running in the high 80s, you will find that bass will not be avidly feeding — especially the bigger ones. But, as you drift along the river, in specific areas you may get several hard strikes from good bass. Check the location where you offered your fly. You may find that at that spot there is an underwater spring of colder water spewing up from the river floor, perhaps where a spring branch is entering the river, and where, consequently, you can have good fishing even in very hot weather.

But, this same area may not be an effective strike zone when water temperatures are rising or falling in the spring and fall. Nearby waters may be closer to the optimum temperature.

On the other hand, in the winter, when temperatures in the river drop below 40 degrees, a spring entering the river, or one emitting water from an underground source, might be a good place to offer your flies (ground water sources are about 50 degrees, so the area near the spring source will be warmer). You see, in very cold weather the metabolism of bass around a spring water source would be faster and consequently the fish would be feeding more frequently.

In short, locate underground water sources if you can. In very hot or very cold weather they can produce bass that are feeding more avidly than in surrounding waters. This is just one example of how understanding water temperature, and how it affects the feeding attitudes of bass and other fish species, can improve your fishing success.

One of the major differences between smallmouth and largemouth bass is that smallmouths are almost always found near or on a bottom that has rock, stone rubble or gravel. Largemouths will locate on such bottoms, too, but they seem to prefer a more silty or even muddy bottom. For example, smallmouths don't seem to be able to successfully live and reproduce in tidal estuaries, where the bottom is often thick muck. Yet, largemouth bass find this kind of place a prime habitat.

And, smallmouths prefer clear waters. It is unusual to find a good smallmouth population in a murky water habitat. In any watershed where there is a portion that is clear and another murky, you will rarely find the smallmouths in the dirtier water. But largemouths will gravitate to such areas, and in fact thrive in waters where it is difficult for an angler to see more than two feet or so into the depths.

OVERLEAF: *Bass fishing in the backcountry of Florida.*

CHAPTER TWO

TACKLE FOR BASS

Other books in this Library series have delved pretty deeply into fly-fishing tackle, but I think a brief review of the basic tackle needed for bass fishing certainly would be worthwhile. Then I'll be exploring specific tactical situations where more specialized tackle should be employed.

RODS

The size of rods used for bass can range from 5 to 9-weights. The lighter rods should be used only in very special situations, such as fishing small streams with smaller flies.

I think the best all around rod for smallmouth bass is an 8-weight, and for largemouth bass, a 9-weight would be my preferred choice. However, there will be situations where a rod slightly heavier or lighter could be used to advantage. Though, it would be rare that anyone would ever need a rod that throws a line heavier than a 9-weight in bass fishing. That is not to say you can't do it, but just that it is more practical and more comfortable to use a lighter outfit. Keep in mind that one of the requirements of many bass fishing situations is repetitive casting, so the angler should use tackle that will most effectively deliver the fly to the target with the least expenditure of energy.

For many years a myth existed that rods to be used in casting bass bugs should have a slow action. In fact, some manufacturers labeled such rods with a "bass-bug action" designation. Today, there are still many casters (and some manufacturers) who believe a slow-action rod is the best bug casting tool. I believe that is simply not true.

What you do want is a medium-fast rod. Keep in mind that a bass bug is air resistant, and the more speed you can generate in the cast, the easier the bug will be to throw. Also, you will remember from my casting lessons that the faster you move the rod tip through a short distance, and the quicker you stop the tip, the greater the velocity of the line and the fly. But slow-moving rods tend to throw big loops, and don't stop quickly — two major faults when you are trying to toss air-resistant popping bugs.

And as I have said many times about fly rod construction, for the fly line to shoot properly, well-designed rods should have large guides, with the stripping (or butt) guide for rods as large as size 7 or larger to be at least 16 mm in diameter. On my heavier rods (size 8 and up), I prefer a stripping guide with a diameter as large as 22 mm.

REELS

Fortunately, reels for bass fishing don't have to be as complicated or expensive as those required for fly fishing for many other species. Neither largemouth or smallmouth bass are known for long runs, although the power of a bass of more than five pounds really surprises someone who has not caught one that large.

I like reels that are light in weight, since in many situations you will be casting all day long, and obviously a lighter reel is less tiring than a heavy one. A good bass reel should have a wide-diameter spool, which permits the angler to crank in loose line quickly. That's important sometimes — especially in a boat — when you hook into a trophy-sized fish.

The drag on a bass reel doesn't have to be particularly good. But, there should be enough restraint on the spool so that if line is stripped quickly from the spool, the spool doesn't overrun and tangle the line.

LINES

The fly line is a critical component of bass fishing tackle. When I was a young man, the only fly lines available to us were floating lines in either double or weight-forward tapers. Somewhat later, shooting heads came on the market. And it was not until the 1950s that manufacturers began manufacturing lines that either sank quite slowly or quite rapidly. Now we have a vast array of fly lines to choose from, and there are some tactical situations in which specific fly line selection can make a decided difference in how effectively you are able to fish for bass.

The one line every bass fisherman should own is a weight-forward floating line. This is the best line choice for more bass fishing situations than all other situations combined. And of all the floating weight-forward configurations that are available on the market today, there are basically two types that the bass fisherman should equip himself with.

One line should be the conventional weight-forward line, which has a relatively long front and back taper and belly section.

The other should be a weight-forward line with shorter front and back tapers, as well as a shorter, extra heavy belly

— a design which is commonly called a "bass-bug taper." This design permits the line to be retrieved closer to the angler so that a pick-up can be easily made, and on the forward cast a fair amount of line can be shot through the guides to the target. *Such lines are for rather close-in work where you are fishing bugs or flies at a distance of less than 50 feet, but want to retrieve close to you.* However, for most bass fly-fishing situations, the conventional weight-forward floating design is still the best line, despite the apparent superiority such a name as "bass-bug taper" might imply. Keep in mind — and this applies to a lot of other fly-fishing tackle, too, I suppose — just because someone has given this line a great sounding name that sounds like it will give you better performance does not necessarily mean that it will!

There are three other specialized fly lines, sink-tip lines, full-sinking lines, and shooting heads, that can be very effective for making special types of presentations and retrieves in certain bass fishing situations.

SINK-TIP LINE APPLICATIONS

When you want to present an underwater fly into a small open pocket of water amid lily pads or other dense vegetation, of course a floating line will not work, because it cannot get the fly underwater. Neither will a full-sinking line (or a line with a long sinking head) be appropriate, because this type line will tend to tangle in the grass on the near side of the hole immediately in front of you.

For this situation, one of the very best ways to catch bass is with a sink-tip line and an underwater fly. Use a Red & White Hackle Fly, a black Lefty's Deceiver or a Woolly Bugger. Cast the fly to the far end of the opening in the grass. The sink-tip line will drag the fly deep into the hole, where it can then be retrieved underwater across

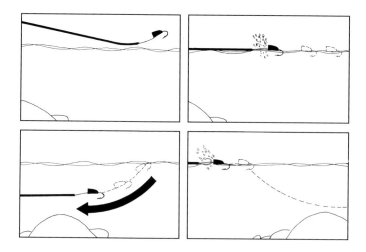

Popping Bug Presentation with Shortened Sink-Tip Line

the width of the hole. The sink-tip line can then be easily lifted from the water for another cast and presentation.

For popping bug presentations, the performance of this type line can be further improved by cutting off the first five feet of the sink-tip portion of the line (which is normally 10-feet long in most commercially manufactured sink-tip lines). This modification allows you to retain some of the characteristics of a sink-tip line, but its shortened tip will cast easier and won't sink as deeply.

When fishing a popping bug with this modified or shortened sink-tip line, use a ten-foot leader. Make your cast into the hole. If you start retrieving as soon as the popper hits the surface, and continue to retrieve, the popper will stay on the surface and pop in the same manner as if you were using a weight-forward floating line. But, make a few strips on the line, causing the popper to pop and gurgle, and then stop. If your pause is long enough, the shortened sinking portion of the line will drag the popper beneath the surface. Once it disappears, start stripping again. As you do, the sinking tip will loft to the surface, bringing the popper with it. As you continue to strip, the popper will again pop and gurgle. Now stop retrieving. The popper will again sink below the surface.

Using this technique you can fish the popper on the surface for as long as you like, then swim it underwater for brief periods, and then repeat the operation. It's a deadly technique for those times when conventional retrieves are failing to produce strikes.

FULL-SINKING LINE APPLICATIONS

Another way to fish a popping bug is to use a full-sinking line and a long leader — at least 12 feet in length. This rig is highly effective when you are trying to draw fish out from underneath a boat dock.

Here's how to use it. Make a long cast and allow the popper to sink to the bottom, or at least to a considerable depth in the water column. Then begin your retrieve. As the stripping continues, the line will straighten and this will cause the popper to dive even deeper into the water. Then stop your retrieve. The line will start sinking, but the popper will begin to float towards the surface. Repeat this retrieve-and-stop method. This will cause the popper to swim forward and up, then down, then up, and so on. Retrieving a popper alongside the pilings of a boat dock with this up-and-down motion is the most effective technique I know for bringing up bass from underneath a dock.

SHOOTING HEAD APPLICATIONS

In those situations when you aren't sure where the fish are holding and you want to search for them with your fly over a large area of water, the shooting head is an ideal tool. The shooting head (as has been explained in somewhat more detail in other books in this series) is a line that has a heavier front portion (the "shooting head") connected to a much thinner line (the "shooting line") behind it.

The theory behind this line design — and it works well — is that after you have built up the required line speed by false casting the heavier shooting head, on your final forward cast the heavy head of the design will easily drag many yards of the extra-thin shooting line toward the target. Thus, the average caster can frequently add as much as 30 feet to his casting distance by switching from a conventional weight-forward floating line to a shooting head, and as a result can cover many more square feet of water in his searching routine.

Incidentally, as I've also mentioned before, you will find that when you use a shooting head, you'll be able to obtain much more distance by switching to a shooting head *one size larger* than the rod manufacturer's specification calls for. Thus, if you are using a rod designed for casting an 8-weight line, go to a 9-weight shooting head.

I'd like to repeat the following for emphasis: in fly fishing for bass, once you have selected a good rod, the most important choice of tackle, aside from the patterns you select, are the types of lines you use, particularly in regard to how line selection influences presentation and retrieving techniques.

LEADERS

Leaders for bass fly fishing are really pretty simple. If you fish for largemouths (and sometimes smallmouths) where there is an excessive amount of aquatic weeds or lily pads in the water, then a straight leader is often best. A single strand of 15-pound-test monofilament perhaps six feet in length is ideal. The grass will disguise the leader, so there is no need for a long one. Such a straight section of leader will not tangle in the weeds, as a tapered leader constructed of varying weights of monofilament connected by a series of knots might do.

In clear waters, for almost all river and lake bass fishing situations, a tapered leader about nine feet long, with a tippet strength testing from about six to 10 pounds, is my preferred choice.

In several other books in this series we have discussed in detail how to construct such a tapered leader. But briefly stated here, in order to build one, you want first to establish what pound-test strength the butt section should be. Then make each succeeding section of the leader one half the length of the one preceding it. Then add a tippet about two feet long. Remember not to use stiff nylon for the butt section!

For example, a very good bass leader for general work is designed as follows: take a butt section of four feet of 25-pound monofilament; to that tie a two-foot section of 20-pound monofilament; to that tie a one-foot section of 15-pound monofilament (giving you a total leader length of seven feet); and finally, to that tie a two-foot section of six to 10-pound monofilament tippet.

When using sinking lines, leaders can be quite short. For many years we fished sinking lines with long leaders which were developed for floating line applications. But bass anglers who now routinely fish with sinking fly lines know that a long leader tends to loft higher than the line when descending to the fish.

They have also learned that shorter leaders will allow you to sink the fly almost as fast as the line. So when fishing a sinking line, only when the water is extremely clear do you need to go to longer leaders. Under most circumstances, you rarely need a leader longer than three feet with a sinking line.

FLIES

Regarding fly selection, while many fly patterns will, of course, work on both small and largemouth bass, I'm going to treat smallmouth and largemouth flies separately, because certain patterns are best suited when fishing for each species.

SMALLMOUTH BASS FLIES

Smallmouths are much more likely to take a small fly than a largemouth, although bigger smallmouths will accept a huge fly, as much as even seven inches in length. And, of course, flies that more closely resemble the natural prey that they feed upon seem to work a lot better for the smallmouth. A good example of this kind of fly is the Clouser Crayfish which is just a fair largemouth pattern, but a deadly one on smallmouths.

Because you'll be chasing tiny to trophy-sized smallmouth bass, in all kinds of watersheds — lakes, rivers, and small streams — in both the shallow and deep water, you will need a variety of flies to meet all the various fishing conditions you will encounter.

But after a lifetime of chasing smallmouth bass, it pleases me to report that to catch these fish most of the time in most situations, you really don't need a lot of fly patterns. Having the right ones, of course, is important, but the number required is minimal. For this reason, I have categorized the flies you will need to catch smallmouths in just about any type of watershed as follows.

One of the most important flies when fishing for any size largemouth or smallmouth bass is the **Clouser Deep Minnow**. It should be dressed in various color combinations. The best colors are those that imitate local baitfish, or one with a white bucktail underwing and a chartreuse upper wing. This pattern should be tied rather sparsely to be effective. For small bass, those under a foot in length, the fly should be tied on #10 to #6 hooks and dressed with either 1/00 or 1/50-ounce eyes.

My next choice would be a pattern that has been mentioned in several of my books — the good, old **Woolly Bugger**. This is a very versatile fly. For small bass, it can represent a leech, a nymph, a streamer, or just something that looks "buggy" and good to eat. The best two colors seem to be olive or black. Hook sizes range from #10 to #6.

And since small bass are great insect feeders, any buggy-looking nymphs, such as the **Gold Ribbed Hare's Ear**, **Red Squirrel Tail** or **Muskrat** patterns are all good. They should be dressed on hooks ranging from #12 to #4.

I also like to always carry an assortment of basic **soft hackle trout** patterns. Dressed on #10 to #6 hooks, these flies can be very deadly, especially if the fish are feeding on emerging insects.

And of course I include another favorite pattern, the **Clouser Crayfish**, which is a superior fly for all smallmouth bass, since it represents perhaps their favorite of all foods. For small bass the pattern should be dressed on hooks from #12 to #6. I will tell you how to fish this pattern later in the book.

And finally I would add a **Lefty's Bug**, which is a bug I developed for smallmouth bass after seriously fishing for them over two decades. It works well on all smallmouth bass ranging from six inches to six pounders. And it is

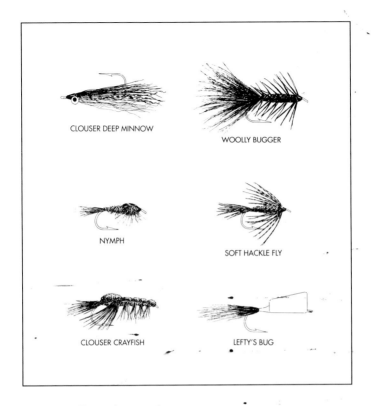

Small Smallmouth Bass Flies

very easy to cast. Its design has several advantages: the materials never foul on the hook during casting; it will pop and gurgle every time you twitch your line; and it lifts easily and quietly from the water on the back cast. Commercial bodies for this bug can be purchased in various colors and sizes from many local fly shops. For small bass, I like this bug dressed on a #8 or #6 long shank bug hook. I believe that the color of a popping bug is unimportant for smallmouths. I often use yellow ones, simply because they are easy for me to see while fishing them.

Fish Larger than 12 Inches

Some of the same flies that appeal to smallmouths of less than 12 inches will take larger bass. Such patterns must be tied much bigger, of course. Remember, while it's true that elephants eat peanuts, they don't make a living off them. If you fish with small flies you will catch mostly small bass. Bigger bass are caught most of the time on larger flies. This is a hard lesson to learn, but it's an important fact that bears repeating: *If you want to catch bigger bass, fish with larger flies*.

Having said that, let me suggest that when you are trying for smallmouth bass (and largemouth bass, too) that exceed a foot in length, most underwater flies should be at least 3-1/2 inches long, and many times flies from 4 to 5-1/2 inches will appeal to bass whose weight exceeds say, two pounds. Consider that a Rapala plug or a seven-inch plastic worm is eagerly attacked by bigger smallmouths. So, a four-inch fly isn't really a large one. Yet, there is tendency for many bass fly fishermen to fish underwater with smaller patterns ranging from 1-3/4 to 2-1/2-inches long. And then they wonder why they catch so few big fish!

Flies previously mentioned that are effective on small bass but that work well on bigger bass are: the Clouser Deep Minnow, Woolly Bugger, Clouser's Crayfish and Lefty's Bug. But a few extra words of advice need to be added when fishing these patterns to bigger fish.

When using the **Clouser Deep Minnow** for bass longer than 12 inches, I favor a #2 or #1 hook and a pattern length of at least four inches. Depending upon how deep I am fishing, I use lead eyes that range in weight from 1/50 to 1/36 to 1/24-ounce — with the 1/36-ounce eyes perhaps the most frequently used. This weight is required to get the larger and heavier patterns down deeper.

Big Smallmouth Bass Flies. From left to right, top row: *Lefty's Bug and Red & White Hackle Fly;* middle row: *Clouser Crayfish, Clouser Deep Minnow, and Woolly Bugger;* bottom row: *In-Line Spinner Fly and Half & Half.*

The ~~Woolly Bugger~~ is certainly a great smallmouth fly. For larger fish I dress the fly on extra long (3XL) hooks from #6 to a big #1. Few people build weedguards into the Woolly Bugger, but when I weight the fly heavily, as I frequently do (either with wire wrapped on the shank or with lead eyes), I add a weedguard, since the fly will be traveling near or along the bottom, many times in heavy vegetation, and needs added protection to prevent snagging. I construct my weedguards of #6 stainless steel trolling wire or monofilament.

I think bass can be made to believe that the Woolly Bugger is a leech, a hellgrammite, a minnow or a crayfish, depending on how it is fished in the water column. For example, a white or gray Woolly Bugger fished like a streamer fly gives a good impression of a minnow.

Every experienced smallmouth bass fisherman knows how this species prefers crayfish to all other foods. So I have tried every imitation of this prey species I could get

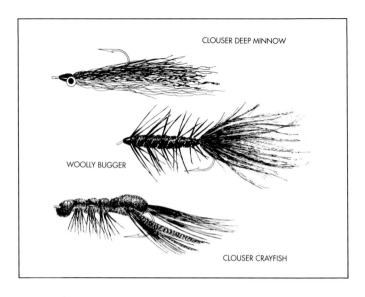

CLOUSER DEEP MINNOW

WOOLLY BUGGER

CLOUSER CRAYFISH

Big Smallmouth Bass Flies

my hands on. While there are many crayfish patterns — and some work fairly well — the Clouser Crayfish is by far and away the best imitation, as far as I am concerned. The Clouser Crayfish should be used in a variety of hook sizes — from #6 to as big as #2/0.

When working the surface with poppers, I prefer Lefty's Bug. For larger bass I mount the body on a #1 hook with a long (3XL) humped shank hook.

The past two seasons I have been using a fly that Bob Clouser designed, which we call the Half & Half. The pattern is really a combination of a Lefty's Deceiver and a Clouser Deep Minnow. The Half & Half has a tail or wing section that protrudes well behind the hook, similar to the manner in which a Lefty's Deceiver is dressed. While most of the time the tail or wing is constructed of feathers, Ultra Hair (a commercial fly-tying material) is also an effective

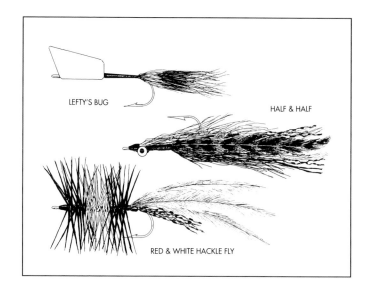

LEFTY'S BUG

HALF & HALF

RED & WHITE HACKLE FLY

Big Smallmouth Bass Flies

material for building both the rear tail or wing and the front wing. A pair of lead eyes is located just behind the hook eye, and then a conventional Clouser Deep Minnow pattern is tied at the forward end of the hook. What results is an extra long fly which presents a big profile that larger smallmouths strike well. (In fact, since I began using this fly in the late 1940s, it has been one of the best producers of strikes on bass of respectable size.)

Until I began using the Clouser Deep Minnow and the Half & Half, the **Red & White Hackle Fly** was my favorite underwater fly when I was after big smallmouth bass. I still use it a great deal. It is especially effective in low light conditions (early and late in the day, and when the water is just a bit roiled). It is a very old pattern, used by bass fishermen since the 1800s. In the 1950s it was called a Homer Rhodes Tarpon Fly. Today, some people call it a

Seaducer. Regardless of the name, the Red & White Hackle Fly belongs in every bass fisherman's fly box.

I have made only two slight changes to the original pattern of the Red & White Hackle Fly. First, I add two or three strands of pearl Flashabou or Crystal Flash to each side of the tail. And if I want to present the pattern deeper in the water column, sometimes I will position lead eyes at the head.

I think it is important to mention that only the combination of the colors red and white seem to yield outstanding performance with this pattern. Long ago, when I found out how very good this fly was, I began experimenting with various colors and blends of colors. To me, some of these flies looked terrific. I remember blending a mix of yellow, yellow-dyed grizzly and natural grizzly feathers that looked fabulous. But the bass didn't vote the way I did. As I have said before, *I think the reason why flies and lures that combine the colors of red and white are such good fish getters is that when a predatory bass (or other species) chases a baitfish, it is usually attacking from below and behind the prey. What the predator sees of its prey, therefore, is a white belly and red gills.*

I also use a **Clouser Crippled Minnow** — a pattern that hangs with its tail down and its head on the surface, imitating a Rapala plug.

CLOUSER CRIPPLED MINNOW

Flies that have a good deal of undulating action can cause largemouths to get interested — fast. Good examples of this are the Water Wiggle Bug and other patterns onto which long extensions of rabbit fur have been tied to the rear of the hook.

When selecting largemouth bass flies, keep in mind that most of the time largemouths will be taken in either the calmer parts of a river, or in lakes. In both places there is little or no current flow, so flies that move well when activated by the angler are preferred. Also, largemouths tend to seek denser cover than smallmouths, both for safety and when in ambush. They will lie among a fallen tree's limbs, or similar thick cover. For this reason, it is always preferable that largemouth flies fished underwater carry some sort of weedguard. We will discuss weed-guards later in more detail.

As with smallmouth bass, you don't need a huge assort-ment of flies to fish well for largemouth bass under most conditions. If you are armed with the following flies dressed on different sizes of hooks, you can fish confi-dently almost anywhere largemouths will be found.

The following patterns (illustrated on the following page) also work well on largemouths: Red & White Hackle Fly, soft hackle flies (for smaller largemouths), Half & Half, Clouser Deep Minnow, and Woolly Bugger.

Surface Flies

A great deal of fly fishing for largemouth bass is done on the surface, because in many largemouth habitats, the dense aquatic vegetation severely impairs underwater fly presentations and retrieves. So let's look first at the surface patterns that work well on largemouths — the poppers, bugs, and divers.

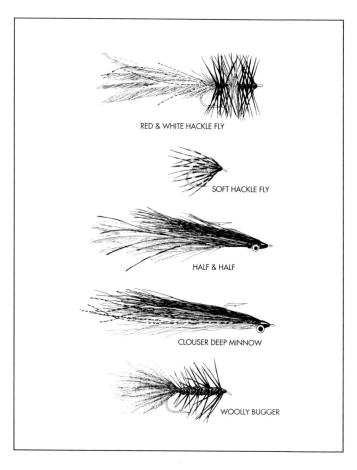

RED & WHITE HACKLE FLY

SOFT HACKLE FLY

HALF & HALF

CLOUSER DEEP MINNOW

WOOLLY BUGGER

Largemouth Bass Flies

If I had to choose only two bugs for largemouths, I wouldn't hesitate. They would be the Pencil Popper and the Gerbubble Bug.

The **Pencil Popper** is very different from all other poppers. It is a thin, sleek bug, designed to imitate a struggling minnow. In fact, it is one of the best imitations of a crippled minnow that I have ever used. Its name is derived from the fact that the designer took a rod made of balsa wood and shoved one end into a pencil sharpener, tapering the rear of the bug body as you would in sharpening a pencil. When fitted with a weedguard (usually a single wire or stub of monofilament angled from the front of the belly toward the hook point), this bug has one advantage over all other surface flies. Because of its sleek profile (a large Pencil Popper is no more than 1/2 inch across the face) you can fish it among lily pads and other floating aquatic vegetation where a bug with a larger face would be constantly entangled. This is a major reason why I always carry Pencil Poppers when fishing for largemouth bass.

The other surface bug choice for me would be the **Gerbubble Bug.** This fly was developed by Tom Loving, who taught the great Joe Brooks how to fly fish for largemouth bass in the tidal waters of Chesapeake Bay. For some reason, this pattern remained relatively unknown for many years, and it has only been during the past decade that sharper largemouth bass fishermen have begun to regard it as a standard surface pattern. And perhaps that's because Dave Whitlock, who has done so much to publicize bass fishing with a fly rod, began to promote the Gerbubble Bug.

There are three styles, or ways, of tying the Gerbubble Bug. This first tying style, which was developed by Tom Loving, produces a rather rectangular bug with neck or saddle hackle radiating out from its sides.

The second style, developed by Dave Whitlock, consists of constructing a deer-hair body on the hook and then adding the saddle or neck hackles.

But the best method of tying the Gerbubble Bug, in my opinion, has been devised by a very innovative angler friend of mine, Norm Bartlett. Norm uses the same body as the first tying design (the Loving tie), but he substitutes marabou for chicken neck feathers or saddle hackles radiating from the sides of the body. What a difference in action this makes! This Bartlett design has always out-produced any other popping bug pattern I have ever used on watersheds where there is no current, such as in lakes, tanks and farm ponds, and where, therefore, the bug should be moved rather slowly. Where **Bartlett's Gerbubble Bug** excels is that after the bug is popped and stops moving, the super-soft marabou hackles suspended below the bug just sit there and *slowly* undulate. I have watched curious largemouths move up under the Bartlett Gerbubble Bug and be triggered into an absolute feeding frenzy by those slowly waving marabou hackles!

Another fine popping bug is what I would call a **Basic Largemouth Popper**. It is usually designed with a round and cupped face, to which are added several soft rubber bands extending from each side, which help induce strikes when the bug is worked in quiet water, performing much the same function as the marabou on a Bartlett Gerbubble Bug, although rubber is not as supple as marabou. Most patterns of the Basic Largemouth Popper have some hackle extending beyond the hook bend. Perhaps more largemouth bass have been caught on this type bug than all others, simply because it is the most popular style being commercially manufactured today.

But there are good and poor designs of the Basic Largemouth Popper. Any popper (used in either large or small-mouth bass applications) is poorly designed if the hook eye is located in the center of the bug face. It is even a worse design if the face is cupped. What makes centering the hook in this manner a bad feature is that half of the bug face is *always* underwater when a back cast is made.

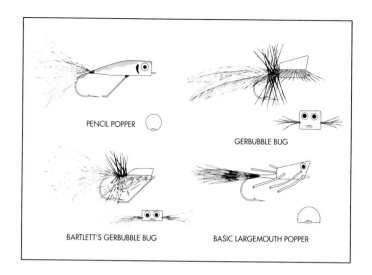

Largemouth Bass Surface Flies — Side and Front Views

This usually causes a loud "blooping" noise that will frighten any nearby fish. *Instead, all well-designed popping bugs should have the hook eye located at the very base of the bug.* Off-centering the hook in this manner also aids in lifting the bug quietly from the surface on the back cast.

The most common poor popping bug design is one in which a number of hackles have been tied in beyond the bug body, splayed apart much like a swimming frog's legs, to which several feathers have been palmered or spiraled around the hook shank between the bug body and the point where the hackles are tied in that outward splay. There are two problems with this design. The splayed and palmered hackles make the bug much more difficult to cast. And these fluffy feathers tied in at the rear of the pattern cause the rear of the bug body to be buoyed up in the water so that the hook rides close to the surface, where it may be missed by the fish on the strike.

One other poor popper design feature is the use of regular shank hooks. The hook point should never sit directly under the bug body. This makes it more difficult for the bass to be impaled on the point. And, short shanks on bugs tend to cause them to sit flat on the water's surface, which means that they don't pop as loudly or pick up as easily with a long line. *Instead, the hook on any popping bug should extend well beyond the body.* Longer shank hooks also cause bugs to tilt (as shown in the illustration below) which results in better hook-ups and easier lifts from the surface.

My favorite largemouth popper is the previously mentioned **Lefty's Bug**. It has a tail of squirrel secured so that it can't foul when casting, and also offers minimal air resistance during the cast. This bug has a slanted front face with the hook located at the rear of the bug, making it easy to lift from the water. The slanted face is superior to a cupped face, and is all that is required to make the noise needed to attract a bass. For largemouths, I use a large Lefty's Bug dressed on a #1 or #1/0 hook with the addition of some rubber bands through the body.

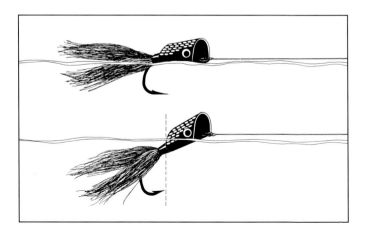

IMPROVED BASIC LARGEMOUTH BUG

A compromise between my favorite largemouth popping bug patterns and the ones most frequently being used today is a design I call an **Improved Basic Largemouth Bug**. This pattern has a cupped face, the hook located at the base of the face, and a tail made of squirrel tail, with rubber bands through the body.

Incidentally, if you would like to add rubber bands to any of your current bug selections, it's easy. Purchase some rubber hackle from a fly shop or fly-tying catalog. This material is simply thin rubber bands. If you can't find that, use the skirt material that goes on any bass spinner used by spin and plug casters. Extra skirts can be bought from almost any fishing tackle shop that handles bass lures. To install the rubber hackle, insert a single strand of the rubber through the eye of a needle. (Try to use a small needle — needles too large will sometimes pop the finish from the far side of the bug body where the needle point exits.) And if you encounter difficulty in getting the rubber hackle through the eye of a smaller needle, simply insert a 1/4-inch loop of 4-pound monofilament through the hook eye. Slip the end of the rubber hackle into the monofilament loop and pull the hackle through the hook eye. With a pair of pliers, grasp the needle firmly and shove it through the bug body. You can combine different colors of rubber hackle, if you wish. And if you use skirts from bass spinner lures, you will find there are a staggering number of colors to choose from.

There are three superb largemouth bass flies that I like to refer to as transitional flies, in the sense that they can be fished on the surface as a popping bug, or underwater, or with a combination of both surface and underwater swimming techniques.

The first is the **Deer-Hair Bug**, which many bass fishermen enjoy and prefer to use in the belief that this fly possesses the special advantage that when a bass bangs into one, because the pattern has a soft and yielding body, the fish will hold on longer, allowing the angler to better set the hook. I'm not sure that this is true.

One disadvantage to the Deer-Hair Bug pattern, as I see it, is that if it is dressed on the same size hook that you might use for Basic Largemouth Bug or Lefty's Bug patterns, it usually ends up being much larger and therefore much more air-resistant on the cast than these other flies. But an even greater fault I find with it is that it tends to soak up water after a bit of use. The fly becomes increasingly harder to cast, and has to be replaced. But despite my negative evaluation, I have to report that thousands of bass are caught each year on this pattern.

I do believe, however, that there is one place where the Deer-Hair Bug is supreme: on lakes around a boat dock. A dock often furnishes superior cover for bass, as it gives the fish good overhead protection and permits it to wait in the shade and ambush any prey that comes near. Recognizing this, experienced lake bass fishermen follow the technique, first, of beginning to fish early in the morning (even just before dawn) when everything is very quiet, and then making their casts so that the Deer-Hair Bug is thrown up on the dock and then twitched off into the water, imitating the typical action of a natural. This is an alluring target to a hungry bass hiding beneath the dock.

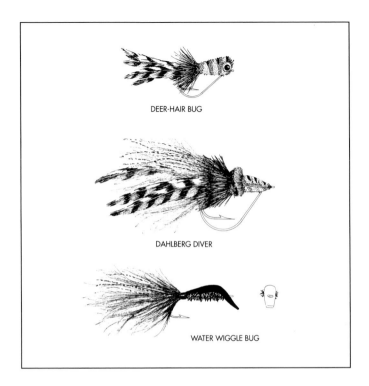

DEER-HAIR BUG

DAHLBERG DIVER

WATER WIGGLE BUG

Largemouth Bass Transitional Flies

In this situation, whereas a typical hard-bodied bass bug would probably make quite an unnatural "clunking" sound when it fell from the dock, alerting rather than attracting the fish, the soft-bodied Deer-Hair Bug, on the other hand, can be dragged off the deck and made to fall silently onto the water without a bass ever realizing a fisherman was nearby.

Next is the **Dahlberg Diver,** truly one of the only new fly designs to be developed in years, a great transitional largemouth fly. The pattern can be fished as a popping bug, a streamer fly, or a combination of both.

It is dressed with a tail of a variety of materials, ranging from a strip of rabbit fur to marabou hackle. It is the design of its head that sets the Dahlberg Diver fly apart from all other patterns. The head is constructed from spun deer hair which tapers from the hook in an upward slant until it joins a hackle collar of the same deer hair. The size of the wing and hackle behind the head can be anything from something as short as two inches to really long wings of six or more inches.

The Dahlberg Diver fishes best if the slanted portion of the head is dressed prior to fishing with a silicone paste, such as Dave's Bug Floatant.

Some people are now making heads shaped like the original deer-hair Dahlberg Divers from plastic closed-cell foam. These are also proving to be very effective patterns.

To fish the Dahlberg Diver, make a cast to the target area. Lower the rod, remove the slack and strip in line, just as you would when working any popping bug. If you make short pulls on the fly line, the bug will make the same noise as a conventional popping bug. Make longer pulls and the bug will pop and dive briefly below the surface. If you make a series of long strips on the fly line, one after another, the bug pops, dives below the surface, and then swims along underwater as you continue to retrieve line. But if you will make a definite pause in the stripping motion, the buoyant bug will float up to the surface. All three retrieving techniques work at different times, making the Dahlberg Diver one of the most versatile of all bass bugs.

If you plan to buy any Deer-Hair Bug or Dahlberg Diver flies, check them carefully. Buy only those in which the hair has been packed very densely on the bug body and trimmed well below the hook so that it will have plenty of clearance to impale the bass easily. On Dahlberg Diver patterns, dense packing also produces added buoyancy so that the fly will not sink and destroy its unique action.

Next is a unique and rather interesting largemouth bass fly, the **Water Wiggle Bug**, developed by Larry Tullis. If you have been lure fishing a good deal, you may be familiar with the Flatfish plug, a lure shaped somewhat like a banana with a hook eyelet located at one end. When retrieved, the Flatfish adopts a near vertical position which creates a very quick back-and-forth wiggle that many species of fish find attractive. Larry's Water Wiggle Bug does the same thing. It is made from a tough closed-cell foam body in the shape of a long rectangle, with a slant on one end. The hook eye is located at the slanted section. The hook rides behind the body on the retrieve and generally carries a marabou or feather tail. The fly wiggles back and forth when the line is retrieved in a long, slow pull, much like the action of a Flatfish. It can be twitched on the surface like a popper, then dragged underwater, where it is also very effective. I understand that the Water Wiggle Bug pattern is now commercially available through many fly shops.

Underwater Flies

The **Lefty's Deceiver** in blended colors (the wing is black and sometimes I make the collar dark purple) is one of the best flies I have ever used when seeking big largemouth bass. It is especially effective in southern waters from California and Texas across the country to Florida. I like to tie the fly at least four inches long, and often will tie it as long as six inches. If you want it to fish three or more feet deep, don't place too much deer hair at the collar. But, if you tie in a lot of deer hair at the collar, it will fish within inches of the surface, buoyed there by the deer hair. I add a number of strands to the wing, either of black, or a combination of black, red, and purple Flasha-bou or Crystal Flash.

All hardware fishermen have learned that in the right hands, the Pig and Jig is unquestionably the finest lure there is for catching the greatest number of largemouth bass, as well as the biggest ones. Nothing on the bass fishing professional circuit or in the experience of thousands of amateur bass fishermen can produce as well as the Pig and Jig — if you have the skill and patience to work it properly, and slowly.

For the fly fisherman, Dave Whitlock has created a fly that works almost as well as the Pig and Jig lure. He calls it the **Dave's Hare Jig**, since it is made of rabbit hide and works in the water like a jig.

Largemouth Bass Flies. From left to right, top row: Deer-Hair Bug, Gerbubble Bug, and Bartlett's Gerbubble Bug; middle row: Basic Largemouth Popper with cupped face, Improved Basic Largemouth Bug, Pencil Popper with mono stub; bottom row: Dahlberg Diver, Pop Lips, and Water Wiggle Bug.

Largemouth Bass Flies. From left to right, top row: *Red & White Hackle Fly, Woolly Bugger, and Soft Hackle Fly;* middle row: *Black Lefty's Deceiver and Half & Half;* bottom row: *Clouser Deep Minnow and Dave's Hare Jig.*

This fly is available through many fly shops and is also produced by Umpqua Feather Merchants (address: P.O. Box 700, Glide, Oregon 97433). Because it is designed to work on or near the bottom, the fly is equipped with a monofilament weedguard. The pattern has a total length of about five inches, more than half of which is a soft, wiggling rabbit fur tail. The hook is dressed along its length with the same piece of fur that forms the tail. Several rubber bands and some strands of Crystal Flash protrude from the sides. At the head is a pair of lead eyes that help it plummet to the bottom and ride and hook up very well. Dave's Hare Jig comes in many colors, but my favorite is the color that best imitates a crayfish, that is, darkish green or brown. However, black and even purple are sometimes effective colors, too. To fish Dave's Hare Jig, you should use a sinking line and a short leader — no

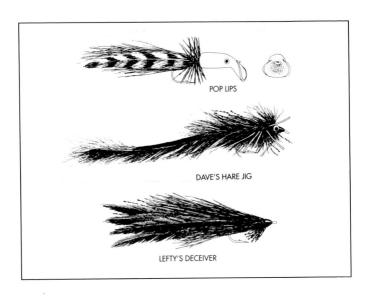

POP LIPS

DAVE'S HARE JIG

LEFTY'S DECEIVER

Largemouth Bass Underwater Flies

more than four feet in length. *Cast the fly out and allow it to sink to the bottom — that's important. This is a fly that works best when it crawls right on the bottom.*

A final largemouth bass selection is another totally new fly designed by Bob Popovics, called the **Pop Lips.**

SOME GENERAL OBSERVATIONS ABOUT THE SELECTION OF BASS FLIES

Several points should be made about tying or purchasing flies for small and largemouth bass.

1) Popping Bugs versus Streamers

Streamers and popping bugs are probably the most widely used fly patterns in bass fishing. The reason for this, I think, is that these type patterns assist in creating the impression to the fish that your offering is a crippled creature, resulting in a higher percentage of strikes.

In many situations, the popper is to be preferred over the streamer, because you can easily manipulate it so that it will appear to be struggling on the surface, as if it were a fish injured or in trouble; while a streamer swimming below the surface — no matter how large it is — must appear to the fish as if it were in good shape and would offer a hard chase if pursued.

Popping bugs also create an illusion that the prey you are attempting to imitate is really much bigger than it actually is, whereas a streamer or other underwater pattern worked in front of a fish can be clearly seen by the fish so that it can determine how big it is, which may not be large enough for its appetite!

And here's another thing. I've done more smallmouth bass fishing than any other kind of fishing in my life. And I have caught a lot of large smallmouth in rivers. But I can't think of a one that weighed over four pounds that I have ever caught on a streamer fly. But I have caught hundreds of big smallmouth over the years on popping bugs.

2) Add Flashabou or Crystal Flash to Your Patterns

The addition of either Flashabou or Crystal Flash (thin strands of mylar) does much to contribute toward strikes. Both tying materials come in many colors. If I were limited to just two, they would be pearl and rainbow. Either of these colors when tied at the sides of a pattern gives off flashes of light that closely imitate a swimming baitfish. But flies can often be made more effective by adding a blend of several colors of Flashabou or Crystal Flash. For example, if the pattern has a white body and yellow wing topped with peacock herl, add some pearl to the white area and some gold Flashabou or Crystal Flash to the yellow area and a bit of green to the herl.

3) Add Red to the Throats of Your Patterns

As I've stated before, since I believe that bass and other predatory fish are excited by seeing the gills of a pursued baitfish as they approach it from the rear, I like to add a red throat (the part of a fly that imitates the gills of a fish, on the underside of the shank just back from the hook eye) to many of my streamers. While many materials can be used for the throat, I feel that red Flashabou and Crystal Flash are the best materials to create this imitation.

4) Eyes Are Important on Underwater Flies

The size and weight of the lead eyes that are attached to a Clouser Deep Minnow, for example, will determine how deeply the fly will sink. And I believe the color of the lead eyes is also fairly critical. After trying many color combinations — from black and white through yellow and black, or red and yellow and black — I have settled on one color combination for lead eyes: dark red. I use dark red paint on the lead eye to cover its entire surface, to which I add a spot of black paint in the center to imitate the pupil. While many paints can be used to tint the lead eyes, I favor Testor's PLA hobby paints.

Currently, the most popular solid weighted eyes are those made from lead, ranging in weight from as heavy as 1/10-ounce to as light as 1/100-ounce. But in response to recent objections to the use of lead in the environment, antimony and tin substitutes, which are about 60 percent of the weight of a lead eye of the same size, have been developed. Also, metal eyes weighing about 75 percent of comparably sized lead eyes are now being made from machined copper.

One word of caution about the use of the heavier lead-eyed flies. When casting them, keep your rod tilted

Lake fishing for largemouth near Mount Shasta, California. ➤

to the side, as it can really smart if one of these guided missiles hits you on your cast. Or, if one hits the blank of a graphite rod, it will frequently cause a costly break.

When you want a fly to sink fairly slowly, weighted eyes made from hollow bead-chain should be used. Bead-chain comes in a number of diameters. If you want a fly with a bulky but not too heavy a head, the largest size works best. A very effective application of these large bead-chain eyes is in night fishing, or when fishing in waters that are a bit dirty and the underwater visibility is so low that even the fish cannot see the fly. They can, however, feel the vibrations that are being produced by the large bead-chain as the fly moves through the water.

Bead-chain is manufactured from brass, chrome-plated steel, or stainless steel. Brass bead-chain gives you a different colored eye, but soon corrodes. Chrome-plated steel similarly will rust after prolonged immersion in water. Stainless steel is, of course, impervious to corrosion, and I recommend it. As far as I know, stainless steel bead-chain eyes are available today only from one source: Joe Branham (address: 802 Northside Drive, Valdosta, Georgia 31602).

5) Add an In-Line Spinner to Your Patterns

During the past year, I have been able to entice some large smallmouths to hit a Clouser Deep Minnow, a Red & White Hackle Fly, a Half & Half, or other standard streamer patterns, by adding an old twist — an in-line spinner blade (illustrated in color on page 45). Many of the earliest bass flies used in the 1880s were constructed with an in-line spinner. I find that larger bass will often hit a fly equipped with a spinner in front, whereas they would ignore the same pattern without it. In-line spinners for flies were readily available in tackle shops many years ago, but now they are hard to find.

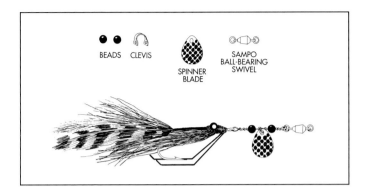

BEADS   CLEVIS

SPINNER
BLADE

SAMPO
BALL-BEARING
SWIVEL

Components and Construction of In-Line Spinner

But they're easy to make. Here's how you do it: You'll need thin stainless steel wire to build the spinner on; a clevis (a U-shaped piece of metal with holes in each end through which a pin or bolt can be run) to hold the spinner blade and permit it to revolve around the wire shank; small glass or plastic beads to position in front and behind the clevis to allow it to turn easily; a gold, silver, or brightly colored spinner blade at a size no larger than about the size of your thumbnail (I prefer the Colorado style blade since it emits the most flash); and the smallest size Sampo ball-bearing swivel to connect to the leader and prevent the line from twisting. If you can't find these components locally, you can purchase them from Netcraft Fishing Tackle (address: 2800 Tremainsville Road, Toledo, Ohio 43613)

The only tools required are pliers with needle nose cutters that will sever wire.

To attach the in-line spinner to your leader so that your line will not twist on the retrieve, make a loop at either end of the wire with a Haywire Twist knot and attach one loop to the fly and the other to your leader.

While in-line spinners can sometimes be difficult to cast on windy days, or with a floating line, I find that with a T-200 or T-300 Teeny Nymph line the rig will cast exceedingly well. The in-line spinner and fly will certainly improve your strike ratio on large fish. *Since I use a sinking line when fishing an in-line spinner, I often build a weedguard of #6 trolling wire on the hook prior to making the fly. This permits the fly and spinner to creep and crawl along the bottom without tangling.*

6) Use Weedguards

In the past several years, I have become an advocate for the use of weedguards on bass flies. As I see it, as more fishing pressure is exerted on bass, they have become more wary and stay closer to heavy cover when not actively feeding. Therefore to catch more, and especially to catch bigger bass, you need to fish with flies that can invade their cover without becoming snagged.

There has been a tendency over the past 20 years to use stiff monofilament as weedguard material. But monofilament offers two drawbacks: first, it isn't as stiff as I would like it to be; and second, after several fish are caught it becomes badly deformed and has to be replaced. Instead, I have been using stainless steel trolling wire (such as that used by offshore big game fishermen). It comes in two colors, coffee and bright silver, and either is okay, as I find that the color of the weedguard makes no difference to the fish. Stainless steel trolling wire can be purchased by the number. For most bass fishing situations, I normally prefer using #5 wire (with a diameter of .014 inches), but when I'm fishing in heavy cover, I'll use a slightly thicker #6 wire (with a diameter of .016 inches).

You can make a weedguard from a single or double-strand of the wire, but a double-strand weedguard is best, I think. This is because it increases your protection from snagging the fly; and if one of the strands becomes deformed after hooking up a few fish, you can twist it back and forth and break off the distorted strand, leaving a smooth end. *Never clip the wire,* since it leaves a sharp point that may cut you. To make the double-strand weedguard, take a piece of 5-inch trolling wire as described previously and bend it in half. Then lash the wire to the underside of the hook as illustrated below.

Note how I've made my weedguard wire extend to the rear of the hook. Most weedguards end near the hook point, but with this special feature, the wire will now collapse easily on the strike. This results in a short lever that the fish must push against before the guard collapses so that the hook point can impale the fish. The longer a lever, the more easily it can be moved.

After you've put together your double-strand weedguard attach it to your fly as shown, at top, in the illustration on the next page. It's important how the end of the weedguard is shaped. It should not end in a straight point. When the fish grabs the fly, if its mouth pushes against the straight end of the wire, there is a tendency for the wire to

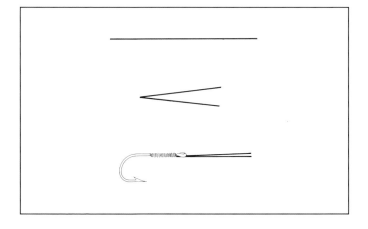

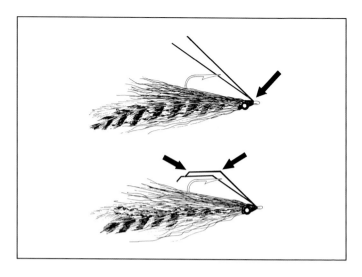

shove the fly away from the fish. Instead, make two small bends in the wire as shown, at bottom, in the illustration above. One brings the tilted wire about even with the point, and the second causes the wire to roll around and downward. When a fish takes this long wire lever, it collapses more easily. This type of wire weedguard is superior to any other type that I've ever used on a fly.

As illustrated below, you can also make a single weed-guard for any popping bug that you already have in your

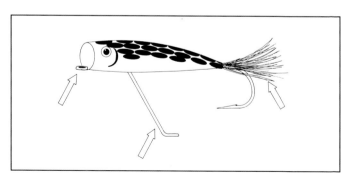

inventory. For this procedure, use a sharp pointed stub of monofilament, preferably about the size of the hook diameter or even a bit larger. Take a needle and insert it at an angle into the bug body. When you withdraw the needle, insert the sharpened end of the monofilament into the hole. Place one drop of fast-setting glue over the point of penetration. The end of the monofilament should be slightly lower than the hook point, and can be bent, as shown, with a pair of pliers.

7) Check Your Hooks for Sharpness

While it's been repeated many times in this series of books, keep in mind that sharp hooks are very important. Many times when a bass takes a bug or popper from the surface, there is a tendency for the buoyant fly to move away from the fish as it strikes. *Of all flies offered to fish, bass flies that work the surface should have the sharpest hooks possible so that the slightest contact of the hook by the bass starts the penetration.*

8) Fish Barbless

Finally, I want to again emphasize that I have been using barbless hooks for almost all my fly fishing (and for all of my bass fishing) for the past 30 years. After many experiments, I have concluded that you can catch more fish on barbless hooks, and obviously it's much better for the fish. That particularly applies to bass, because with their large mouths, they frequently take flies quite deep in their throats, and it is so much easier to remove a barbless hook from a caught fish.

OVERLEAF: *Fishing for largemouths on the Oxbow River, Georgia.*

CHAPTER THREE

FLY FISHING FOR BASS IN RIVERS, LAKES, SMALL STREAMS AND PONDS

INTRODUCTORY NOTE

Just as the tackle requirements for smallmouth and largemouth bass are quite similar, the two species are fished for in essentially the same way. Really the only difference between the large and smallmouth bass, from the fly fisherman's standpoint, is that largemouth bass prefer to exist — and therefore are fished for — in stiller and somewhat warmer waters. So while the following material will principally be discussing the techniques and tactics for fly fishing for smallmouth bass, to simplify things and avoid unnecessary repetition, you may assume that the same techniques and tactics also apply to largemouth bass, except where I have added some special comment that applies only to largemouth bass fishing.

WATERSHEDS FOR BASS

There are three types of watersheds where anglers will find smallmouth bass — rivers, small streams, and lakes; while the principal habitats of the largemouth bass are lakes and ponds.

Each watershed requires essentially the same fishing techniques, but there are some subtle differences that need to be explored.

LARGE RIVERS

To discuss the techniques for fly fishing for smallmouth bass in rivers, I find it is helpful to categorize rivers by size. I define a large river as one in which the average width of the stream is greater than 100 yards; a medium-sized river as one in which the average width ranges from, say, 40 to 100 yards; and a small stream as a river with an average width of less than 40 yards. Smallmouth fly-fishing techniques need to be adjusted for each river type.

Maybe it's because I grew up in the mid-Atlantic area that I enjoy bass fishing on larger rivers more than anywhere else. In this region there are a number of excellent smallmouth watersheds, including such fabled rivers such as the Susquehanna, the Juniata, the New, the Potomac and the Shenandoah. If I had to list at this writing the two best trophy rivers where I have ever fished for smallmouth (and where you can reasonably expect to catch smallmouth bass weighing as much as five or six pounds), I would say they are the James and New rivers in southern Virginia. Likely the proliferation of smallmouth in these rivers is caused by their high mineral content created by deposits made in them by the underground water sources that travel through the limestone faults underlying the entire mid-Atlantic area.

In the northeastern United States, I would have to list the upper Delaware River in New York as a truly great fishery. In fact, New York boasts a number of super small-mouth rivers — such as the Niagara, as does New England. Among the five rivers in Maine that are more than 100 miles in length is the Penobscot, which is a favorite smallmouth river of mine. And there are so many good smallmouth rivers in eastern Canada that it would take an entire volume to list them. In short, through much of the northern portion of the United States and southern Canada, where there are clear flowing, cool, big rivers, you have great smallmouth fishing.

In the Midwest, a number of rivers have been recognized as being superb smallmouth fisheries ever since the sport of fly fishing was in its infancy in the United States — and they are still good today. The St. Croix River in Minnesota, for example, immediately comes to mind. It is one of the best smallmouths rivers I have ever fished.

There are some great smallmouth rivers in the West which many trout fishermen either don't know about or ignore — and that's a shame. The lower Snake River in Idaho as well as the John Day River in Oregon, are superb smallmouth bass fisheries. Smallmouth in these rivers will give you action on a fly rod almost equal to any trout river in the West.

An especially pleasant way to fish large and medium-sized rivers is to drift along and blind cast. You should constantly be on the lookout for any indications of an underwater rock (indicated by a small ripple or "wrinkle" on the surface) and work it thoroughly. Also be on the watch for minnows being chased — a sure sign of a hungry bass. If you will cast a popping bug or underwater fly ahead of the skipping minnow and begin a fast retrieve, you will almost always be rewarded with a strike.

Larger rivers are rather predictable. One of the first things you'll learn about big smallmouths in large rivers is that they rarely hold in the current. What they prefer to do is lie in rather calm water immediately adjacent to faster currents. This permits the trophy bass to burn less energy as it maintains its position in the slow water, but at the same time be in a position to watch and take action when it sees food being brought to it in the current. To accomplish this purpose, the smallmouth seeks structures.

There are many structures in a river that a smallmouth will utilize for cover or as an ambush spot. Among the most preferred are rocks, logs and sunken trees (especially those with the root system still intact), and grassbeds, such as willow grass or lily pads which offer perfect habitat for locating food sources, especially minnows.

Rocks — Smallmouths prefer rocks above all other types of cover. Nothing attracts them more. It can be a single rock, a ledge or a series of rocks. Understanding the shape of individual rocks and their relationship to smallmouths is a vital key to success.

In flowing water, a choice spot for a smallmouth is where there is a relatively calm current, and shade from an overhead rock that permits the bass to hide and wait without working too hard to look for approaching food.

Perhaps the most productive rock formation for the angler is one where a ledge extends outward from the river bank. If the ledge is joined at the bank, this type structure will create a small body of quiet water on the downstream portion of the rock. The deeper the water behind the rock, the more safety will be offered for the bass and the more likely that it will be there — or that a larger one will soon occupy the spot. If water flows a few inches over the ledge in its downstream journey, so much

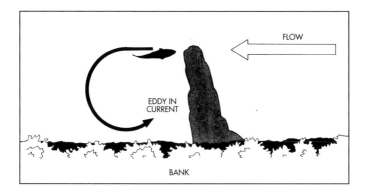

Ledge Extending Outward from Bank

the better. If the ledge tilts downriver, forming a minor roof in the quiet water where a bass can feel safe from overhead danger, then you have one of the most choice spots to seek a bass in the river.

Another superb location to find smallmouth, especially when they are feeding, is a rock or ledge of rock lying at right angles to the current and *slanting upstream* as illustrated, at left, below. As it projects outward and upward from the river floor, such a rock formation causes a dead or still spot as the water pushes in against it. Shade and overhead cover are supplied by the slant of the rock. Here a bass can wait in calm water, unafraid of predators, in a position to see all prey and food that is being brought down to it by the current as illustrated, at right, below.

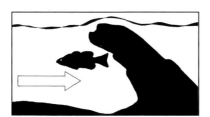 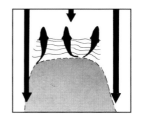

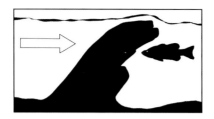 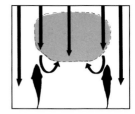

A less desirable, but still productive, ledge formation is one that is at right angles to the current but *slanting downstream*. Such a ledge offers the same comfort and protection as one slanting upstream, but this structure prohibits the bass from seeing approaching food until it sweeps past the rock as illustrated, at left, above.

For that reason, to get a better view of approaching food, a bass will almost always be located on the downstream side and either on one side or the other of the ledge formation, holding in the calm water behind the rock until it starts to feed, at which time it will reposition itself very close to one edge of the rock so that it will be better able to see food sweeping by in the water's current as illustrated, at right, above.

Any rock that slants downstream will almost never have a bass holding on the upstream side of the rock. The current created by this type structure would force the bass to be constantly swimming to stay in position. In such a case the bass will always be on the downstream side of the slanted rock, where an eddy or calmer current exists.

Any rock that has a shadow under it is a potential place to work your fly. It is always a great place to check out.

When you locate such rock structures, how the fly should be fished is critically important. One fall I caught 39 large river smallmouths on flies. I got most of them from very few locations, because one of the things that I learned was that how the fly swims to the fish is a very important factor in success. In some cases it was best to throw from an upstream position. In other situations more strikes were forthcoming if the cast was made at a different angle.

I have concluded that there are at least two principal factors that determine how the fly should approach the rock formation where a bass is likely to be hiding.

First, as I have emphasized in other books in this series, flies should *always* represent prey species and therefore, *no fly should ever appear to be attacking the bass!* Make sure that the fly comes to the fish *naturally*. Crayfish imitations should not, for example, swim swiftly upriver and directly at the bass. Minnows should not be retrieved very rapidly with long sweeping pulls on your fly line, as most of the time minnows hold in the current, drifting back a few inches, moving around rather slowly unless pursued. Try to duplicate this action with your retrieve of minnow imitations.

Second, if there is shade on one side of a rock, then the bass will most likely be on the shady side, all other things being equal. If any current exists, it is best to position yourself so that the fly can be offered as if the current were carrying it towards the bass. The poorest presentation is one in which the fly swims from a downstream angle upcurrent and towards the fish.

I cannot over-emphasize how important it is to understand the relationship between smallmouths and rock structures in the river.

Wood — Wood is another important structure for smallmouths. But it's not as attractive to them as it is to largemouth bass. However, where rocks don't exist, wood is the smallmouth's next most preferred structure. Wood includes sunken trees or trees that are half submerged, pilings (especially those that have been in the water a long time), and boat docks (which, of course, may not always necessarily be made of wood). Of all the wooden structures that exist in a large or medium-sized river, a submerged tree that still has some of its root system intact is the most productive for smallmouth. In flowing water the root section will usually be upstream, and as the roots catch or dig into the bottom, the main trunk swings directly downstream.

Another favorite wood structure for the smallmouth is a single log that has one end resting on the bottom of the watershed and the other end either lofting upward, or actually protruding above the surface.

Many fly fishermen fish a log or submerged tree trunk improperly, or at least not in the most effective manner, in my opinion. They tend to fish the fly at right angles to the log or submerged object.

In a large or medium-sized river it is best to get into position downstream and just a little off to one side of the log. Anchor your craft so you can retrieve the fly without having the current push against it and influence the action of your fly as it is being retrieved.

(And keep in mind, it is always best to fish a weedless fly around logs, particularly if they have any projecting branches.)

Make a cast that is well upstream from the log on the same side as you are anchored. If you are using a popping bug or a surface fly, begin your retrieve.

If you are fishing an underwater pattern, allow the fly to sink so that when you retrieve it, it will ride at the same level in the water as the log. Do this several times. If there is no strike, permit the fly to drop deeper so that it is fished almost on the bottom and under the log.

To fish the other side of the log, it is best to reposition your boat so that you can work along the other side. A

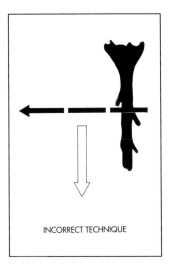 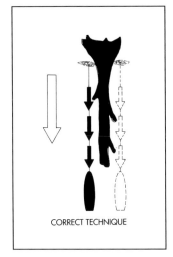

INCORRECT TECHNIQUE   CORRECT TECHNIQUE

Incorrect and Correct Techniques for Fishing for Bass by a Sub-merged Tree or Log

mistake often made is to anchor directly below the log and fish down each side.

You'll get a decent retrieve this way, but if the bass takes the fly you may have a serious problem, because in these circumstances the fish will have an opportunity to dive under the log and entangle your leader. By staying on one side, if a strike occurs, you can apply rod pressure, hopefully to pull the fish away from the log.

If you encounter a log stuck in the bottom, with one end projecting either toward or above the surface (as shown at top of next page), don't make the mistake frequently made by many anglers: they cast at the most visible and obvious end of the log which is riding highest in the water column. But because bass inevitably prefer safety and shade, they will almost always be positioned at the *other* end of the log, the one nearest the bottom.

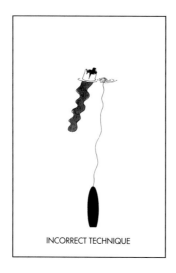

INCORRECT TECHNIQUE

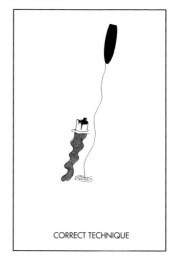

CORRECT TECHNIQUE

And again (as shown below), don't fish at right angles to the log. Instead fish this log the same way you would the submerged tree, by getting on one side, retrieving and then moving to the other side and repeating this routine.

On bright sunlit days, boat docks and submerged wood structures are always best fished on the shady side. Where there is considerable current, the fish will frequently be in front of the structure, or along one side at the projecting edge — just as they position themselves around rocks.

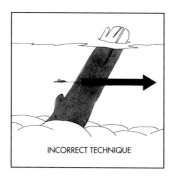

INCORRECT TECHNIQUE

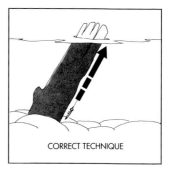

CORRECT TECHNIQUE

Grassbeds — In any river (or lake), a prime place to offer your flies to smallmouths is near grassbeds. The characteristic grassbeds found in rivers are not the deep underwater patches of vegetation found in lakes, but rather those that form along the banks, islands and shallow bars. Most of the time the roots are in the water, as the grasses can survive well if they grow on the river bottom just out of the water.

Willow grass (an aquatic grass that grows to a maximum height of perhaps 18 inches, with leaves shaped like those of the willow tree — hence the name willow grass) is the most prolific river grass in the United States. It is the habitat for many creatures that smallmouths eat, including two of its favorite take-out meals: minnows, which are seeking safety from the bass among its dense strands; and crayfish, which are themselves in the grassbeds feeding on plant material and small organisms that have attached themselves to the grass.

The most productive grassbeds for fishermen are those in which one or more sides of the vegetation drops off into water more than a foot deep. Such vegetative structure is always a good bet. Willow grassbeds that grow in just a few inches of water are generally not too productive, as smallmouths rarely feed in such shallow depths.

But, grassbeds grow only during the warmer months. During the very late fall, winter, and early spring, grassbeds will only present a three to five-inch stubble, but even this stubble can be productive throughout the dormant months, as minnows will still seek shelter there.

There are two hot spots for grassbeds. If there are narrow indentations — from a few feet to as much as 30 feet — along the edge of the grass, these will be hot spots that should always be patrolled with your flies. And on almost all grassbeds, the very best spot will probably be where the bed forms a point. Make it a practice always to check out any section of grass that extends into a point away from the main bed.

Use of Boats, Motors and Anchors on Rivers

On most large rivers you can use boats powered by motors and make a moderate amount of noise or disturbance and get away with it. But the smaller the river, the more stealth and quiet you'll need to exercise on your approach.

For larger rivers I prefer to work from an aluminum jon boat which has a large capacity and permits me to carry all sorts of gear. I like those which have at least a 42-inch bottom, which makes them much more stable. A jon boat's flat bottom is not good for cruising on rough water — as is often encountered when fishing lakes — but on rivers it is preferred because its bottom contour allows you to get into very shallow water. And there are times when the ability to fish in water less than 18 inches deep is a decided advantage.

For many years, jet-drive engines were considered to be a suitable motor only on big western, Alaskan, and New Zealand rivers. But lately there has been a revolution in thought about this. Now, many of the top midwestern and eastern bass fishermen working the larger rivers are using jets instead of propeller-driven engines. Jet-drive power allows you to traverse shallows, snake your way through riffles and in short, fish many waters formerly off limits to anglers with propeller-driven boats.

My second choice for fishing larger rivers — and all other smallmouth waters where a boat is required — is a canoe. It has disadvantages in that it can be tipped over rather easily, and has a limited amount of space to pack gear on board. But, offsetting that is the ability to sneak

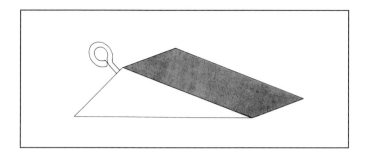

Mule Anchor

up on bass in a canoe. Nothing beats the quiet of a canoe approach to smallmouth, except wading.

I prefer a special anchor for my jon boats. Unfortunately, you'll have to make your own, as I don't know anyone who manufactures them. This anchor is called a mule anchor, made from lead. Look at the illustration above and you can see that it has maximum gripping power for its weight. Usually a mule anchor weighing no more than 12 to 14 pounds will easily hold a 16-foot jon boat well, even in swift water. The advantage of the mule anchor is that while rock-filled river bottoms can often cause the conventional anchor to snag on the bottom, making it almost impossible to free it, the mule anchor has a slanted face that holds well and yet releases easily. Simply move upcurrent of the anchor and the boat's wedge-shaped bow will slide backwards and away from any rock it may be snagged on.

You make a mule anchor by constructing an anchor-shaped form with a large piece of sheet metal — bent into the shape. Into the center of this form, insert a short steel rod which will serve as the anchor's hook. Then fill the receptacle with hot lead and as soon as the lead has hardened, cut away the sheet metal.

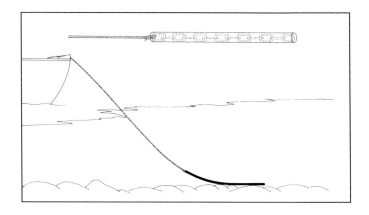

Drag Anchor

One of the problems that is frequently encountered when drifting along a river is that the boat tends to turn in the current or the breeze; whereas for maximum control, you really want to have your boat moving across the surface at a straight angle. When I don't have an electric motor, I use another type of anchor, a drag anchor, to accomplish this purpose. The drag anchor is simply a length of chain (usually 1/4-inch diameter links, although heavier chain can be used on larger boats) which is inserted inside a section of plastic tubing. As illustrated above, one end of the chain is attached to a rope that is then connected to the boat or canoe. The slower you want to drift, the more rope is paid out. The chain drags on the bottom, causing the craft to travel bow first. This works well, even in deep water lakes, as the chain suspended well below the boat or canoe acts just like a sea anchor.

For a canoe, I make an anchor by placing a horseshoe-shaped piece of 1/4-inch metal rod in an empty cat food can. The can is then filled with lead. Such an anchor weighs about five or six pounds, an ideal weight for canoe work. *But never tie this anchor to the side of the canoe.* People have lost gear or even drowned by tying the anchor rope to the side of a canoe. In this position, when the anchor catches on the bottom, the pull of the weight is to the side, which will often cause the canoe to tip over. Use a device that lets you suspend the anchor at the very end of the canoe, so that when anchored there will be a safer pull on the craft. Attach the anchor rope *to the rear of the canoe point,* preferably through one of those small anchor holders that are manufactured for small boats. Follow my advice and you'll avoid disaster.

It may seem that I'm paying too much attention to anchors when fishing rivers. But the anchor is one of your most important tools when fishing for smallmouth bass in such waters, because getting quietly into position so that the correct approach and cast can be made is vital to consistent success.

SMALL STREAMS

There is a special art to fishing small streams. And, while you rarely catch a huge smallmouth bass in one, there are many other benefits to such a pleasant sport. I confess that I spend several days every year wading small local streams, not because I'm going to catch big bass, but because it is simply so much fun.

There are hundreds of small streams throughout the United States that are best fished by wading. Most are too small or shallow for floating a boat. The most enjoyable time to fish such waters is during summer (roughly from June until mid-October in most areas), although in some southern states you can have fun all year long.

The tackle needed is minimal. An old pair of sneakers (or better, a pair of wading shoes with felt soles) is all you'll need for wading. While some pools may be too deep to wade, most of the streams are negotiable. I also favor a good pair of polarized glasses, since many times you'll be able to see the fish before the cast.

As for tackle, rods from size 5 to 7 are ideal. You'll need only a floating line. Leaders should be from eight to nine feet long, with a tippet of four to six pounds. A small box that will carry a dozen or so flies and a spare spool of leader material will complete your tackle needs. I always bring along a pair of hemostats, since many of the fish will be small, and hemostats aid in removing hooks from fish with a minimum of trauma.

A very pleasant way to spend the day with a friend is for the two of you to wade together, taking fishing turns as you move from pool to pool.

I learned a good lesson many years ago concerning how to fish small streams. I drove to a bridge and let my friend out. Then, I drove downstream and parked the car at a good pull-out spot. This particular stream ran in the shape of a large gentle bend. I walked across the bend to a spot downstream about a half mile away. Working upstream, I was able to fish about one-half mile of water, as did my friend fishing in the opposite direction. Late in the afternoon we met at the car and compared fishing experiences. I had caught a terrific number of sunfish, rock bass and quite a few smallmouths. But my buddy — who was a good fly fishermen — had done poorly.

I thought about that for some time, and during that summer began experimenting. I would fish a certain stretch of water by fishing upstream, and then, after giving the water a decent rest (about a week or two), I would fish the same stretch downstream. I did this several times on several local creeks, alternating upstream and downstream approaches. It wasn't long before I realized that when you fish small streams, you will do infinitely better if you fish upstream. I really have no idea why. Whatever the reason, by the end of that summer, I became firmly convinced that *you shouldn't wade and fish downstream in small creeks.*

As I devoted more and more hours to small stream fishing, something else became apparent, too. I began to notice that the pools in small streams will generally contain one or more rocks, but not necessarily large ones. My friends and I began calling them "cover rocks," because we found that more often than not, the cover rocks in a pool — especially in long open pools — will be one of the best places to locate a smallmouth bass. As a result of this observation, we then started making it a point to work our flies carefully around such rocks, and were often rewarded for our care and patience.

When they are actively feeding in small stream pools, the biggest fish will usually be found at the front or head of the pool, perhaps because the nymphs, hellgrammites, leeches and other creatures that live in or under the rocks in an upstream riffle are first washed down into the head of the pool.

A less productive — but still good — holding position appears to be the tail or end of the pool where water is beginning to be funneled before being emitted downstream from the pool, and where, therefore, any food contained in the current flow will be concentrated. For this reason, you should never step into the tail of a pool. Instead, stay back from it and cast your offerings into the very lower edge. It is often quite surprising to discover how large a bass will hold in such very shallow water. Whereas, if you ignore this technique and step into the pool, you may very well flush such a holding fish, which will likely swim upstream and alarm all the other fish in the neighborhood.

One of the great pleasures of fishing small streams is that you can catch not only smallmouth bass, but also several species of sunfish, rock bass, fall fish and other species that cruise these waters.

All the flies listed for bass less than 12 inches long are effective for fishing small streams.

If you have been a big bass fisherman all your life and haven't sampled some of these small streams, try it during the warmer months. I think you will come to agree with me that it is one of the most enjoyable ways to spend a leisurely summer day.

Most of our natural smallmouth lakes are concentrated in the upper portion of the United States and in Canada. But since so many large dams have been constructed throughout the country, particularly in the mid-South, a large number of terrific and accessible smallmouth bass fisheries have been created in these artificial impoundments.

(The mitigating factor in these watersheds, of course, is the water temperature. In those lakes where summer water temperatures don't reach into the high 80s too frequently, there are good chances of a decent smallmouth bass population.)

In the rest of the country, there are numerous smallmouth lakes extending from Minnesota east through Maine and north into southern Canada, which boasts literally hundreds — or perhaps even thousands — of smallmouth lakes.

Some lakes produce intense hatches for brief periods, and if you are fishing when such a hatch occurs, make a note of the time and water temperature. The chances are excellent that next year at the same time and same water temperature you'll again find the same exciting fishing. Of course, that's one good reason for booking a guide for smallmouth fishing, because they will have local knowledge of such emergences.

Points of land that run from the shore of a lake toward deep water are valued places to fish. *The best points are those that don't descend too quickly into the depths, and which have a bottom formed of small rubble or broken rocks.* Such a bottom is a perfect habitat for crayfish, the most preferred food of smallmouths. If the point extends out into the lake to a water depth from eight to 12 feet, and

OVERLEAF: *Late evening bass fishing on Loch Raven, Maryland.*

then drops to 15 or 20 feet, trophy bass will often lie along the demarcation line between these depths.

In lakes, one of the very best places to score well on all bass is to locate any rocky bars or uprisings from the lake floor that are well away from shore. Find a shallow (less than 15 feet deep) rocky bar that is surrounded by deep water and you have an excellent bass location throughout the spring, summer and fall. Such a bar is especially effective if there is small rock rubble mixed in, as crayfish will hold onto this type bottom.

Another fine place to search for bass in lakes is in those places where the shoreline is composed of broken rock that has formed on the bank and then runs well down into the water. Such structure offers hiding places for the prey species and good ambush spots for bass. This is a good place to cast weedless flies, which allow you to probe all the tiny pockets in the rocks.

Just as in rivers, a host of aquatic grasses — lily pads, pepper grass and many other varieties — flourish in lakes in the summer, often growing from the lake bottom all the way up to the surface. Crayfish, minnows and other smallmouth prey hide among the dense strands, peering out at the bass cruising the outer edges of the grass seeking to become better acquainted with them. This is also true in the winter, when grassbeds can really be the only decent cover for bass and their prey.

FARM PONDS

Farm ponds, most of which are too warm to support a breeding population of smallmouth bass, are a principal domain for largemouth bass. Throughout much of the East and Midwest there are thousands of such ponds. Numerous state records and many, many trophy large-mouth are caught in these ponds every year. There are a number of reasons why this occurs. Many farm ponds are lightly fished — when they were first constructed the farmer often enjoyed fishing them, but as time passed they were ignored. Also, farm ponds have an abundance of food, mainly in the form of bluegills and other panfish. And water in the ponds often stays warm for a long period of the year — giving its entire food chain, including big bass, a longer growing season in which to feed and increase in number and in size.

Every once in a while someone catches a truly huge largemouth from a farm pond. Frequently, this is a pond that was once fished hard until the fishing pressure became so intense, and the catches less frequent and smaller, that anglers ceased fishing there. Then much later on, after the pond had been ignored for several years, some lucky angler came along, cast into it, and hooked a trophy. So if you know of a pond in your area that was once an excellent fish producer but in everybody's opinion has since declined in value, go back and give it a shot — you may reap a handsome reward!

Many years ago the U.S. Department of Agriculture distributed to farmers a pamphlet, written by a fishery biologist, advising them on how to control an overabundance of bluegills in their farm ponds. But the pamphlet actually became a textbook on how to fish a farm pond for either bluegills or bass, because it explained in detail how bluegills move to the shoreline of a pond well after the sun rises, remain there most of the day, and then retreat back to deeper water in the later afternoon. And it further explained that *largemouth bass do just the opposite.* That is, bass stay in deep water throughout the day, and then move to the shoreline in the late afternoon.

To reduce the overabundant population of bluegills, the biologist advised the farmer to wait for a windy day, and then after the sun was up, spread a toxic chemical along the shoreline. Bluegills swimming into this contaminated area during the day would perish. However, throughout the balance of the day, the wind-disturbed shoreline would agitate the waters and slowly dissipate the toxins, so when the bass arrived at the shoreline late in the afternoon or evening, the water was safe.

After reading this booklet, I began making my own observations, which naturally concurred with the scientist's. This told me exactly how to fish for largemouth bass in a farm pond: work the shorelines early in the morning and late in the evening; and during the brighter daylight hours fish the deeper parts of the pond.

Also, farm ponds will more often than not have an overflow pipe which is sometimes called a stand pipe. This overflow or stand pipe, usually located at the deeper end of the pond, offers a good holding and ambush spot for hungry bass. So always fish the stand pipe.

Or if there is a pipe on the shore bringing water into the pond, this is also a choice spot, as minnows will congregate around such an inflow of water, which means bass will probably be there too.

If a pond has a tree along the shoreline, you can just about count on a bass holding nearby. The tree's leaves provide excellent shade, its roots provide a good ambush spot, and its limbs hold insects that will frequently be dropping into the water.

Rocks lining a shoreline are also a prime place to fish, since this is one of the few places where crayfish and minnows can actually hide from bass.

Several fly patterns are deadly in farm ponds: a black Lefty's Deceiver, the Red & White Hackle Fly, the Bartlett's Gerbubble Bug, the Water Wiggle Bug, and one of the very best, the Pop Lips.

There is a right and wrong way to fish a farm pond. Much of your fishing will be working your flies along the shoreline. You should walk the perimeter of the pond with the water on the side from which you normally cast. Thus, if you are right-handed, you should have the water on your right side (as shown at right above). The reason for this is that you will then be casting so that your line travels over water, not over grass and brush on the shoreline where your fly can become snagged (as shown at left).

Farm ponds located in the central and northern parts of the United States can yield bass during daylight hours in even the very hottest part of summer; but nighttime can be the best time to fish these waters, as once darkness arrives, the biggest bass will often prowl right along the shoreline. The best flies for this work are popping bugs, worked gently and slowly along the pond edges and around structures. Another good fly is a heavily dressed Red & White Hackle Fly that will pulsate and emit vibrations in the water that attract bass. I can't emphasize too much how effective night fishing on farm ponds can be during the heat of summer.

THE SEASONS OF THE BASS

There are three distinct fishing seasons for smallmouth bass — summer, late spring/early fall, and cold weather. Of course, the major difference among these seasons is water temperature, although the length and intensity of light is to some degree a factor. During each of these seasons the bass feed differently, and even the size of the fish you may expect to encounter is governed to a large degree by the season in which you will be fishing.

SUMMER

Because most fly fishermen try for smallmouths during the summer months (sometime in June through sometime in September — depending, of course, upon your geographic area), I'll begin this discussion by explaining how to catch smallmouths during the warmer months of the year.

Summer is the time of year when smaller bass are most active. Until a smallmouth reaches three inches in length it feeds mostly on microscopic organisms. After it has reached about three inches in length and until it attains a length of about one foot or so, it is primarily an insect feeder. A typical meal might include terrestrial insects that fall to the water — grasshoppers, aquatic moths, damsel and dragonflies, etc. — as well as all types of underwater creeping, crawling critters — hellgrammites, many kinds of nymphs, leeches, dragonfly larvae, etc. Small bass will also avidly feed on baitfish in many forms, including various minnows and sculpins. But regardless of the fish's size, a smallmouth will always go after any crayfish that it believes it is big enough to handle.

Because small bass are constantly feeding in the warmer months of the year, the summer fly fisherman

98

who enjoys catching this size fish is in angler's heaven. During this time, even on large rivers, it is possible to catch a lot of smaller bass on trout tackle. *In fact, bass from three to 12 inches long feed in quite a similar fashion to trout, but are not as difficult to fool.* If you enjoy trout fishing with a light fly rod, you can have a ball on such smallmouth bass. And they will fight a great deal harder than trout of similar size do.

When fishing lakes or large-to-medium sized rivers in the summer, always be on the lookout for surface feeders. Once water temperature gets into the mid-60s, aquatic insects will be hatching throughout the summer right into the early fall. One clear hatch indication will be the appearance of small rings on the surface caused by the bass reacting to the emergence of flies — either drifting on the surface or taking wing from it.

Unlike trout, bass don't usually hold in a specific spot, but usually cruise about slowly looking for emerging insects. This is especially true in lakes where the current is rather slow.

When the bass spots an emerger, it moves under the insect and *sucks* it in, producing a subtle ring, but rarely a splash. Because the bass is moving, the fly caster needs to get into action quickly, make a cast a few feet upstream of the ring, and drop his fly to the surface as soon as possible after the ring is seen.

It is almost never necessary to match the hatch when fishing like this. Any small offering that has life-like characteristics (hackles that move, soft fluttering hair or similar materials in the fly) will usually work.

Good fly patterns for this type of action are various soft-hackled flies, small Woolly Buggers and nymphs. If anything is considered to be a deciding factor, it is the size of the fly. You'll find that sometimes a pattern tied on a small #10 hook is needed; while at other times a fly dressed on a #6 hook will produce better results.

The bass may be also taking emerging insects that have not reached the surface, but are being captured just underneath the water, and are close enough so that the distinctive ring will still appear on the surface as they grab the insect. If fish are taking insects close to or on the surface in this fashion, many times a small popping bug, dressed on a #6 or #8 hook, *worked quietly,* works exceedingly well. Color of the pattern is almost never a factor as far as the fish is concerned — it's more important that the angler use a color he can see.

What is critically important is that you cast accurately and close to and slightly upstream from the ring. And, that you do it as soon as possible after a ring appears. Wait too long and the fish may have cruised away from the area where the ring was formed.

In many rivers and lakes the greatest number of insect emergences will occur during the last hour or two before dark (and sometimes after dark, which will do you little good since most of this type fishing is sight fishing).

In the mid-Atlantic area, the White Miller mayfly hatches on the major limestone rivers in late July and into August. During these hatches, insects occur in such incredible numbers that the bass often become so stuffed with natural food that for several days immediately thereafter fly fishing can often be poor.

The White Millers hatch out, mate, and die in a period of a few hours. The hatch begins about an hour and a half before dark, when you'll begin to see a few rings on the water as the smaller bass start taking nymphs. Then as the number of White Millers hatching increases, the river often becomes dotted everywhere with rings of rising fish, so that as dark approaches the water will at times be literally covered with the white bodies of the dead and dying insects. Bass (as well as other species) go on a rampage during such a hatch, sometimes cruising about with their heads partially above the surface. They remind you somewhat of a snow plow as they cruise about, mouths open, until they get their fill of White Millers. Then, they dive below, swallow their load, and return to the surface.

Even big three and four-pound smallmouth bass are triggered into feeding when the White Millers are at their peak of emergence. These larger bass seem to lie back and wait until the hatch is really thick, then they, too, begin actively feeding. Often the feeding rings of big bass are not distinguishable from those of small five or six-inch fish.

Of all the insect activity I have ever seen while bass fishing, this is the most dramatic and exciting. There are many mid-Atlantic anglers who can't wait for the White Miller hatch each summer.

During the White Miller and other intense insect hatches, fly fishermen do much better than anglers using artificial lures — even those using very small surface lures with ultra-light spinning tackle.

Many people tie fancy imitations of the White Miller or other similar emergers, believing that they produce more strikes, but that has not been my experience. I find that during these prolific hatches smallmouths are so turned on that many fly patterns will do well. In fact, during the White Miller hatch, my best fly over the last three decades has been simply a #8 barbless hook with a 3/4-inch white marabou tail. The hook shank is dressed with white spun deer hair and trimmed to about 1/2 inch in diameter. The fly is cast to feeding bass and worked in the surface film. Because the fishing is frantic, after I have caught eight or 10 bass, the fly will begin to sink. And while it will still catch fish, it doesn't do as well as when it breaks the surface while being retrieved. So for added buoyancy, I pre-coat the deer hair with a paste floatant. And I will also have six or eight pre-coated flies handy to replace the sunken ones as needed.

Some of the most enjoyable times I have ever had have been fly fishing with light tackle to rising bass that rarely exceeded 12 inches. And what a pleasant surprise it is when every once in a while, a much larger bass takes your fly! Perhaps this bigger bass is remembering its youth and reliving a childhood experience.

During the summer, bass are scattered throughout a watershed. They may be holding in deeper pools, working the grassbeds, or cruising near the surface. This is a good time to search for fish, using a floating line. And the longer that you can make your casts, the more water you are able to cover and the more bass will see your fly. On most watersheds — excluding very small streams — the workhorse for this type fishing would be either a weight-forward 8-weight floating line, or a similarly sized shooting-head rig. If you are fishing primarily for small bass, are willing to limit your casting range a bit, and won't be throwing heavier flies, you can go as small as a 7-weight line, I think.

Great summer places to fish for bass are along rocky shorelines or riverbanks that have a good deal of cover in the form of logs, fallen trees, or a rock rubble bottom. In fact, one of the most effortless and pleasant ways to fly fish for smallmouths is to drift along and cast to the various structures along the bank.

Using a floating line is almost always best for this technique, and the Clouser Deep Minnow, Woolly Bugger, Red & White Hackle Fly and Lefty's Bug are all productive patterns for this kind of bass fishing.

The late spring and early fall seasons are quite similar in that at these times the bass move to different waters and act differently than they do during the summer months. Insect hatches are fewer. In fact, in the spring there are virtually no insects available to bass. In the fall there are still some around, but their numbers decline drastically as the season progresses.

In the fall, both largemouth and smallmouth bass instinctively realize that during the coming long, cold winter there will be little food available, and because their metabolism is slower at that time, they won't have the ability to chase prey species swiftly. So their bodies put out an urgent "Eat now!" signal to enable them to add a layer of body fat that will last them through the winter. And in the spring, since over the winter they have exhausted their supply of stored body fats, their body sends out a similar "Eat now!" command.

During the summer months larger bass feed only sporadically, remaining hidden in cover much of the time. But with the advent of spring or late fall, both little and big bass are actively feeding. This a peak time for fly fishermen, for the bass are still in fairly shallow water and on the prowl.

In the spring when the water temperature reaches 50 degrees, and in the fall as it drops down toward 50 degrees, just about all the bass in a watershed (lake or river) will be feeding more actively than at any other time of the year.

Bass will scatter throughout the watershed as temperatures drop from about the high 60s to 50 degrees. In these conditions, you should still employ a floating line, and summertime flies will continue to work well.

But do carry a fly rod rigged with a sinking line — I prefer to use a fast-sinking line with a leader of no more than five feet long. By fishing a Clouser Deep Minnow, a Half & Half, a large Woolly Bugger or a Red & White Hackle Fly, you can score on those fish that are holding or feeding in the deeper water. When using a sinking fly line, it's best to fish it with a wire weedguard. That way if the fly travels over the bottom or encounters debris or grass, you won't spoil your retrieve.

In early spring one of the best places to work your fly is around old grassbeds. High waters and perhaps drifting ice have broken off the dead grass stems, leaving a carpet of stiff stubble. It is here that minnows try to hide from marauding bass. If I had to choose one favorite spot to work a fly in the spring, it would be such grassbeds.

COLD WEATHER

In fly-fishing terms, cold weather is what I define as the period when the water temperature has dropped below 55 degrees until it reaches the high 30s. This is an excellent time to fish for big bass. It has been my experience in chasing smallmouth bass for five decades that when water temperatures reach about 50 degrees, you rarely catch a smallmouth that is less than 12 inches long.

Where the small fish go, or why they stop feeding, I don't really know. But, I do know that this is the time to seek big smallmouth bass. This is the trophy season. This is the time when you stand your best chance of catching one or more smallmouth bass exceeding three pounds during a day of fishing.

In every area of the country that is inhabited by smallmouths, during this time there will be a few experienced anglers who consistently land bass larger than four pounds, and who will occasionally take fish that top five pounds. I have caught a number of three to five pounders when water temperatures were as low as 38 degrees.

Once you understand the techniques, really big bass can be taken rather consistently when water temperatures range from 60 to just below 40 degrees.

There are some subtle tricks to catching these trophy bass, but almost anyone can master the techniques. *Most important is that your fly be on or very close to the bottom of the watershed most of the time. And, just as important, your retrieve should be much slower than the speeds at which you retrieve when water temperatures are higher.*

Fishing Large Rivers in Cold Weather

Unlike lakes, the structure and environment of larger rivers (those that average more than 50 yards in width) are essentially the same everywhere. And once you understand how to fish one large bass river, the same techniques apply to all others.

In winter, wood — a sunken tree, a boat dock, a log, or any other wooden structure — continues to be a good place for smallmouth bass to hold for use as an observation or ambush spot, although, again as in the summer, I would say that wood is usually a second choice after rocks. And, trees that have a number of large limbs are preferred to a bare log.

In fishing a tree or log, don't forget the right and wrong techniques we discussed earlier in the book. When fishing a sunken tree try to position the boat so that you can make a cast that causes the fly on the retrieve to travel parallel to the main trunk or limbs; and in colder weather, concentrate on getting your fly down to the deepest portion of the log. By fishing such structures when water temperatures are below 60 degrees, anglers have a good chance to score well on big bass.

OVERLEAF: *Smallmouth bass fishing on the James River, Virginia.*

On rivers, when water temperatures are between 40 and 50 degrees, there are two special locations where you often find concentrations of large fish:

1) *On willow grassbeds* that grow on gravel bars with their roots in the water. Here you have a choice spot. When rains cause the rivers to rise so that the grassbeds are covered with two or three feet of rather *clear* water, minnows and crayfish tend to hide among the strands of submerged grass, thus creating a choice habitat for trophy smallmouth. The bass will generally lie on the downstream side of such grassbeds where there is an eddy or quiet water. *Be sure to fish only the downstream side of these grassbeds unless there is an eddy or calm place alongside one of the beds.*

2) *In mini-eddies* created by a rock protruding outward from the bank, a tree that has fallen into the water, or an indentation in the shoreline. As the river current flows rapidly past such places, a small eddy — perhaps only the size of your boat or a little larger — is created. Big river smallmouth bass will frequently prefer these holding locations to all others in the river. Anchor or use an electric motor to hold your boat just off these eddies and fish tight against the shoreline. The trick is to get close enough so that the swift current passing by the eddy doesn't affect your retrieve. *Such areas are best fished when rivers are running from three to six feet higher than normal, and when the water is clear enough to see your fly at least two feet below the surface.*

Two of the best flies for this kind of work are the Clouser Deep Minnow and the Half & Half (both dressed with 1/24-ounce lead eyes at the head of the fly or equipped with an in-line spinner). *When you are fishing in cold weather, all flies should carry weedguards and be dressed with a good bit of Flashabou or Crystal Flash.*

The trick with these flies is to use a fast-sinking line, such as the Teeny T-300, which will easily cast the flies and dredge them along the bottom. Make your cast and permit the fly to sink to the bottom, then slow-crawl it along the bottom. Strikes are often very subtle, so concentration is important.

Fishing Lakes in Cold Weather

Unless you spend a lot of time on a specific lake, you may have difficulty finding big smallmouth bass in a lake, as every lake has its own distinctive characteristics and bottom contours that must be learned. Consequently, fishing lakes in cold weather requires some adjustments to technique.

Be sure to keep in mind the major differences between river and lake watersheds: first, that rivers have a constant current whereas lakes don't; and second, that rivers transport much of the food to bass, whereas in lakes, either the bass have to cruise to find food, or lie in ambush — usually the latter.

This is especially true of largemouths. Instead of wasting considerable energy searching for food, largemouth bass will more likely lie in wait. For that reason we need to understand the types of structure in lakes and how this relates to the way bass capture their prey there.

As previously described, both smallmouth and largemouth bass will use rocks on the bottom for cover when they can. Perhaps one of the best flies for working a rocky bottom is Dave's Hare Jig. Also good are the Half & Half, the Woolly Bugger, the Water Wiggle Bug, the Pop Lips, the Red & White Hackle Fly and the Clouser Deep Minnow. It pays to experiment with all of these flies, since on some days and under differing conditions a particular one will outfish the others.

Unless you are in a wilderness area, where you find a lake you will find people using them for recreation — which means boats — and which, in turn, means boat docks. The docks on most lakes are either fixed or floating structures extending well out into the water. But some docks are constructed with wheels that ride on small rail tracks so that they may be rolled up onto land during the winter freeze-up. The *rails* laid down in the lake bed for these movable docks are a prime site for crayfish. Dave's Hare Jig is an ideal pattern to work along the bottom of the lake where the rails have been laid.

Again, fixed and floating docks are also superb sites for bass, as they provide overhead shade, cover from predators, and a nice hideaway from which to ambush prey that come by. Usually the best time to fish docks is early in the morning, although late evening (and even after dark) can be productive.

Of course, during the daylight hours there is often a lot of activity going on around the docks. This doesn't frighten the bass, in fact, they're quite used to it. But it does substantially retard their eagerness to feed.

Underwater flies, such as the Clouser Deep Minnow, the Half & Half, the Woolly Bugger, the Pop Lips and the Water Wiggle Bug, are very effective around docks, logs and other structures that extend well offshore.

While I would much rather fish for bass with hard-bodied popping bugs, deer-hair poppers will certainly catch you more fish when fishing around docks, as I discussed earlier in the book.

Grassbeds are more prevalent in lakes than they are in rivers, and for the fly fisherman, grassbeds in lakes possess the added advantage of being in water shallow enough for the sunlight to penetrate to the bottom, putting the fish within visual range.

Again, when working lake grassbeds with flies, it's best to arm them with weedguards. And because a lake bed may contain a number of hidden grassbeds, while a depth finder can be a useful piece of equipment for the river fly fisherman, *it is an essential tool for the lake fly fisherman.* One benefit this machine can provide — aside from spotting fish underwater — is to locate unseen grassbeds lying well below the surface. With a little work, you can plot the dimensions and contours of the beds in order to be able to fish them more effectively.

Almost always, underwater grassbeds are fished best when you work the outside edges; and best of all are the points or fingers of the bed that extend out from the mass of vegetation. Flies like the Half & Half, Clouser Deep Minnow, Water Wiggle Bug, Dave's Hare Jig and the Woolly Bugger (which is often perceived by fish to be a leech, which are abundant in some lakes), are all useful flies to work deep around and near grassbeds.

Grassbeds also grow all the way up to the surface of a lake. Lily pads are an excellent example of this. It's always best to first work the outside edges of such grassbeds. Indentations are also good places. *When the skies are very bright and clear, the bass — especially largemouths — will often retreat deep within the grassbeds. At such times you will want to search your flies through all the small open pockets in the weeds.*

Bass in such thick grass also grab a lot of food from the surface, and they are always on the hunt for anything crawling on top of the water. But since conventional surface flies, like a wide-faced popping bug, will often tangle in lily pads and other aquatic vegetation, a better pattern for this type fishing is a Pencil Popper equipped with a monofilament or wire weedguard. A Pencil Popper rarely has a face wider than 5/16-inch. It is a long and sleek pattern, resembling the body of a minnow, which will draw strikes as it slinks snag-free through the lily pads. Another good fly to use when thick vegetation covers the surface is the Dahlberg Diver. When fishing for largemouths, I use them in pretty large sizes, dressing them on hooks as large as #1/0 to #3/0.

Lakes normally don't have any constant flowing currents, but in most lakes the wind creates currents for brief periods of time. While wind is consistently regarded as the enemy of the fly fisherman, particularly because it makes casting more difficult, the wind is your friend when you are fishing a lake. It is a major fish producer. *Realizing the importance of wind is a critical factor in becoming a skilled lake fly fisherman.*

I believe, for example, that as wind-generated waves crash against a shoreline they oxygenate the water and stimulate bass feeding. More importantly, the tiny organisms that baitfish feed upon will be pushed by the breeze toward the shoreline. And as the baitfish follow their food source towards the shoreline, the bass will be following right behind. I can't over-emphasize how important this can be in locating bass. *Because just as trout face upcurrent to watch for approaching food, on windy days bass will hold on a windward shoreline, facing into the direction of the wind.*

In similar fashion, bass will hover in ambush along the windward side of log jams or grassbeds to grab baitfish that are foraging along the edges of these structures, feeding on the plankton and other minute underwater food sources that are being pushed in that direction by the wind. That is, if the wind is coming from the west, bass will locate themselves on the west side of structure, facing east. Usually, the best flies for this type fishing are those resembling baitfish. A Clouser Deep Minnow in a color to match the local minnow population is super for this work.

One of the best places to fish in a lake is the point at which the current of a small stream is entering and continually bringing food into the lake in its water flow. During cooler periods of the year this current is often warmer than the lake; and during very hot periods of summer, it is cooler — both temperature variations that stimulate bass to feed more. Usually at the mouth of such streams, the current will also have created a shallow bar and a drop-off into deeper water. This is superb habitat for feeding bass.

SPECIAL RETRIEVING TECHNIQUES FOR BASS

To the fly fisherman coming to the sport of bass fishing for the first time — particularly the dry-fly trout fisherman who has trained his hands and eyes to master dead-drifting techniques, bass fishing will present some new and interesting technique challenges, particularly as regards to retrieving the most productive bass flies — popping bugs and streamers.

With bass, for example, retrieving the fly across the current is almost always better than retrieving from a downstream to an upstream angle — particularly for underwater flies. On a smallmouth river, fishing an underwater fly upstream will generally result in a snag on the bottom.

But as in trout fishing, sometimes the best retrieve is almost no retrieve. This is especially true with the Clouser Crayfish. With this fly, best results usually come when it is cast slightly upstream and across the current and allowed to drift naturally. The fly will sink slowly and tumble in the current, presenting to the bass the appearance of a crayfish that is being washed downstream by the current. Properly fishing this particular pattern is almost like fishing a plastic worm. You have to watch the line and *concentrate*. If you see the line move unnaturally, or stop, or if you have just an inkling that a bass has taken the offering, strike!

The Clouser Deep Minnow is often dead-drifted in just the same way. Most of the time it is best to cast this fly up and across the stream and permit it to sink a little. Then begin a slow-strip retrieve, activating the fly to imitate a minnow moving contentedly along.

When fishing the Woolly Bugger you can work it as you would a Clouser Minnow, dead-drifting it or stripping it back. Both methods work and both should be tested for existing conditions.

There are varying opinions about how to retrieve a popping bug. The correct procedure is never set in stone, for sometimes a very slow retrieve, combined with a speed-up of the bug, now and then, is best.

What usually governs how fast a popper should be retrieved involves the species of bass sought, what the fish is doing at the time (Is it chasing bait or lying in wait?), and the condition of its watery environment. On rivers, popping bugs should be popped constantly in moving water, because if you pause in your retrieve routine, your bug will be silently drifting, ineffectually, over a lot of fish down in the rocks on the bottom of the river. So in that environment, keep the popping bug moving.

But this retrieving method should not be used when you go after bass in a southern, warm water impoundment, particularly if the water is calm — like largemouths in a Texas tank, for example, where temperatures may be in the mid-80s. These fish will not respond to a popping bug like a smallmouth lying behind a rock in a cool Minnesota lake, I can assure you! There are lots of times in those conditions when actually letting the bug sit for a long time in a dead-drifting position underneath or on the water, with no manipulation by the angler whatsoever, is the preferred technique. What is critically important to realize is that when you are fishing a popping bug, you will have to always modify your retrieve for existing species and fishing conditions.

When fishing any popping bug for bass, many fly fishermen develop a bad habit of working the fly with the rod tip. As they flip the tip of their rod upward to activate the bug and then drop it back down, line slack occurs before it can be removed by stripping on the retrieve. Frequently bass will strike while the slack is in the line or leader — and the fish is missed. If you flop a rod up in the air, it's unbelievable how far the fly leaps through the water and more importantly, how unnatural this movement looks to the fish! Charley Waterman, myself, and several other outdoor writers began writing in the 1950s about not flipping the rod tip when retrieving the popping bug. Still, most fly fishermen continue to do it.

The correct way to work a popping bug with a fly rod is to point the rod at the fish, with the tip just under the water or within inches of the surface. To activate the bug, strip the line. Mix the pulls on the line between short, medium and long ones.

Also make various pauses and then a few quick strips, which permit you to make the bug skip along, rest or just slow-move over the surface. The value in using this method is that all slack is kept from the line and when the fish hits, it does so on a tight line.

An additional fault that many anglers make is to strip the line, drop it, place their hand *forward* of the hand holding the rod, and then grasp the line again. Now in order to strip again, they must release the line from their rod hand and place it back in that hand again, thereby losing control of the retrieve for a brief period of time.

The retrieve should instead be made by stripping back line with the line hand. As you make your strip, bring your line hand up and *behind* the hand holding the rod and line. That way you always have control of the line. And by varying the speed of the strips from slow to fast, with a pause in between, you can vary the retrieve so that the line remains taut. *You should always keep the rod tip pointed at the fish and never manipulate the fly with the rod when you're retrieving a streamer or any other underwater pattern.*

And as Dave Whitlock mentioned in talking about bass fishing in one of our symposiums, when a fly is 60 feet away, or even 40 feet, the person manipulating that fly has no idea what it really is doing. At that distance, almost everybody over-exaggerates their stripping action, making very long strips instead of short ones. Dave reports that in his fly-fishing schools it is very difficult to get across to a lot of people that a one-inch strip means a one-inch strip! Because as we all know, little creatures like aquatic insects generally don't make big, dramatic moves.

NIGHT FISHING FOR SMALLMOUTHS

Smallmouth bass feed at night during the summer, and it has been proven many times that just like big brown trout, smallmouth bass can often be caught more easily at night, in both lakes and rivers. And that's particularly true during the hot summer months.

There are at least two advantages to fishing at night for smallmouth bass. First, in relative darkness the bass will tend to move into water that is much more shallow than the water where they spend their time during bright sunlit days. And second, when bass are in the shallows at night, they are actively feeding — after all, that's why they are there in the first place.

A floating line is the best choice for night fishing. I use a rather short leader, simply because it tends not to tangle as much as a long one.

Since at night you are casting blind and everything has to be done really by feel, if you are going to do much of this kind of fishing, you need to keep in mind a few basic casting principles. You will recall that for good casting technique, it is important to pick up the correct amount of line, make a single back cast and then shoot line and fly to the target . . . that if you bring in too much line you will have to make one or more inefficient false casts to get it back out . . . or that if you pick up too much line, the cast may be ineffective. Also, that since each person's skill level differs as to how much line he can pick up effectively, each person has to make his own determination, based upon his own casting ability, of the exact amount of line he should carry outside his rod tip to make effective casts.

Keeping all those principles in mind, since at night you cannot see your fly or line, and therefore cannot see well enough to monitor and adjust your casts, here's an old but simple trick you can use that I believe will help you greatly. During the day, go to your selected fishing water and make a number of casts. Determine how much line should be outside of your rod tip for you to make your most effective back cast. With that amount of line extended from your rod, make a mark on your line at the point where it is adjacent to the fingers of your stripping hand. Bring the line home and tie a nail knot into the line at that designated mark with 10 or 12-pound monofilament. Be sure to pull the nail knot securely into the line's finish and clip the two ends of the remaining monofilament closely.

At night, as you retrieve line, you will feel a slight bump as the nail knot passes across the fingers of your stripping hand. This is easily felt, but never interferes with fishing or casting. As soon as you feel that bump, make a back cast and come forward and shoot line, secure in the knowledge that you are casting at your most effective distance. This is an invaluable aid to fly fishing at night, and it can even be helpful to beginning or inexperienced fly fishermen when they are casting in the daytime.

For safety reasons, you should only wade areas that you know are easy to traverse and where there are no deep drop-offs. The best places are where the lake or river floor is even and no more than hip deep. And it's always a good idea to have someone else fishing with you, too. You can't be too careful at night. And even though it is dark, don't be *in the dark*. Always check out and become familiar in advance with any area you plan to wade or fish at night.

I have had my best luck when fishing on moonlit nights, although a few anglers I know who are skilled at it believe that very dark nights with little moon are best. Perhaps I do better because I can at least partially see what I'm doing in the moonlight.

One of the best flies I have ever used for night fishing for smallmouths is the Red & White Hackle Fly. To make the pattern as bulky as possible, I have as much hackle spiraled around the hook shank as I can tie on. With such heavy hackling, the fly pushes more water, putting out stronger vibrations that bass can detect. If there is much grass or I'm forced to fish quite close to grassbeds, I dress the fly with a double-wire weedguard.

The trick to retrieving this fly is to move it in slow, foot-long strips that cause the fly to sweep a foot or so through the water. Then, make a definite pause to assist the bass in finding the fly. Continue to repeat this retrieve over and over.

When a fish is hooked you may need a light to land and release it. I use one of the small flashlights (powered by one or two AA batteries) which usually come with an eye on the end that I can tie a loop of cord to. I hang this loop around my neck, so that it is easy to grab the light when I need it. Also, some camping suppliers now sell a great light for working around the wilderness campsites at night. It has a headband which allows you to carry it on your head or hat. Such a light is especially handy, since it frees both hands.

Whenever you use a light while fishing, don't point it at the water, and use it as little as possible.

Finally, I have to confess that while I have done enough of it to know how to go about it, I don't enjoy night fishing very much. For me, fly fishing should be a visual game.

OVERLEAF: *Dean Butler with a huge Niugini bass, taken on a fly.*

CHAPTER FOUR

THE EXOTICS

PEACOCK BASS

When most fly fishermen think of bass, their thoughts naturally turn to smallmouths and largemouths. But there are two other bass-like fish that are far larger and more exciting. One of these is the peacock bass, called *pavon* by the natives in most South American countries where this magnificent fly rod fish lives. As Harry Middleton mentioned, the peacock actually isn't in the bass family, but is cataloged among the genus cichlids which abound throughout the tropical waters of South America.

Until a few years ago few American fly fishermen knew about this great fish. But lately, anglers have been traveling to the jungle rivers and lakes of South America in search of it. Those who have caught peacocks have become totally addicted to chasing them.

In most areas where you fish for peacock bass, you will find three different species: the royal pavon, the butterfly pavon and the peacock pavon. Of the three, the peacock pavon is the largest. It is thought to reach a top weight of 30 pounds, and anything exceeding 15 or 16 pounds on a fly rod is considered a true trophy. Each subspecies is marked slightly differently. Perhaps the butterfly (a fish that rarely exceeds 10 pounds) is the most colorful. The royal pavon prefers to live in faster river currents than the other two species. A really large royal pavon will weigh as much as 10 pounds.

The best fishing I have ever had for peacock bass is at Manaka Lodge, in Venezuela, located about two miles downstream from the junction of the Orinoco (one of South America's largest rivers) and the Ventuari River (after the Orinoco, Venezuela's largest river). No fish I have ever encountered in fresh or brackish water makes such an explosive sound as does the peacock bass when it takes a prey, fly, or lure on the surface.

I recall one time when Gene Mueller (outdoor editor of the *Washington Times*, and an old friend) and I were fishing in a shallow lagoon of the Ventuari River. It was dead quiet and only the jungle birds interrupted the silence as we fished along a shoreline. Suddenly we heard a loud popping sound around the bend. The closest way I can think of describing it to you would be to suggest it would be similar to the sound made by someone about three feet away from you blowing up a paper bag and suddenly slamming his hand into the bag to burst it. Gene and I looked at each other in complete surprise and asked the guide what in the world had made that noise. He explained that a pavon had hit something on the surface.

Then he quietly maneuvered our boat around the bend, and at a distance of about 150 yards away — that's the length of one and a half football fields — we could see a spot of foam spreading on the water. We realized that even from that considerable distance, the sound we had heard had been as loud and clear as that of a snook (famous for the loud popping sound it makes when it strikes prey on the surface) taking something from just a few yards away!

Gene was casting a sleek spoon on plug tackle and I suggested that he cast in the vicinity of the foam. On his third retrieve, as the lure traveled by a sunken log, we saw a bright fish slash into the spoon. Gene hooked up the fish and finally boated a peacock bass weighing in the 13-pound range.

That was my first exposure to the awesome sound a peacock bass makes in taking a surface offering, and even though I have heard it many times since, I will never forget that first one! No freshwater fish I have ever tried for anywhere in the world makes such a loud and startling noise as the peacock bass.

There are a number of habitats that peacocks live in, and each one requires slightly different fly-fishing techniques. From a technique standpoint, deep-water lakes are probably the least interesting habitat in which to fish for peacocks, especially if there is a lot of standing timber. In such an area, the peacock's behavior is much like that of a largemouth bass. It tends to hover very deep in the water column among the thickest timber. This permits it the maximal opportunity for ambushing its prey while remaining hidden from danger. The only effective way you take these fish on the fly in these deep-water lakes is to use full-sinking lines and drag a weedless fly close to and through the drowned trees. While some nice fish can be taken with this technique, it lacks the absolute rush of adrenaline you get when fishing for peacocks in water less than 10 feet deep.

When Les Adams, publisher of this Library, and I arrived at Manaka Lodge a few years ago, the lodge personnel told us that while we could catch peacock bass on fly-fishing tackle, large plugs would be much more effective. I was willing to bet, however, that this assessment was based upon their experience with the fly fishermen who had preceded us there, who were using giant 12-weight tarpon rods to present very large, heavily dressed flies tied on big hooks. That's a rig that's hard to cast under even the best conditions, and in the heat and humidity in that jungle, I'll bet those fellows were through for the day — at least as far as fly fishing was concerned — after only an hour or two!

During the week we were there, Les and I experimented with many types of flies and plugs, and concluded that if we presented the right patterns, we could actually be more effective with flies than with plugs — especially when we were fishing in very clear water, which was really most of the time.

There are some good reasons for this, I think. First of all, many times the fish would spook when a heavy plug crashed on the surface, whereas a fly alighting quietly on the surface not only didn't alarm the peacocks, in some cases it actually attracted their interest. There were also situations when if the right fly could be retrieved very slowly and teased along in front of the larger and more wary peacock bass, the fly's slow, undulating motion really turned them on. And since a properly tied fly much more closely resembles a natural baitfish image than does a hardware plug with several dangling treble hooks, it is more effective in clear water conditions.

But we found the best pattern to fish for peacocks on shorelines and lagoons was a Lefty's Deceiver. I tied up a number of Lefty's Deceivers that had a total length between five and eight inches — peacocks do want a large image to strike. *But, I dressed the flies on a relatively small #1/0 hook, which made the flies so much easier to cast and allowed us to use somewhat lighter and less tiring rods.*

We found that the best color combination for our Deceiver patterns was a white wing with some pearl Flashabou or Crystal Flash, a white bucktail for the collar, and *a topping that ran from the hook eye more than halfway back of the fly in either Ultra Hair or bucktail in a bright*

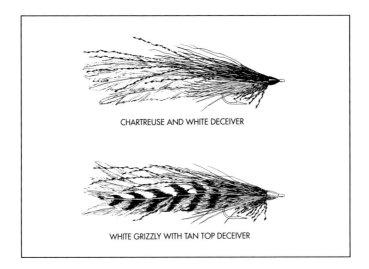

CHARTREUSE AND WHITE DECEIVER

WHITE GRIZZLY WITH TAN TOP DECEIVER

Peacock Bass Flies

chartreuse color. Another pattern that worked well was a Lefty's Deceiver dressed with a white wing and Flashabou or Crystal Flash (as described above), but with a natural grizzly feather on the outside on each side of the wing, with a topping or either light tan or gray bucktail. On all Deceivers, a throat of red Flashabou or Crystal Flash seemed to draw more strikes.

All three species of peacock will take popping bugs (I like the Galasch type which is a classic saltwater pattern) and Dahlberg Divers on the surface — especially when the water is dirty or clouded by rain. Color does not seem to be important. Frequently, the peacock bass will hover near fallen trees, sometimes tight against the shoreline. In these situations, a Dahlberg Diver fished with a weed-guard is deadly.

In the Orinoco and Ventuari — as in many South American rivers — there are places which are referred to

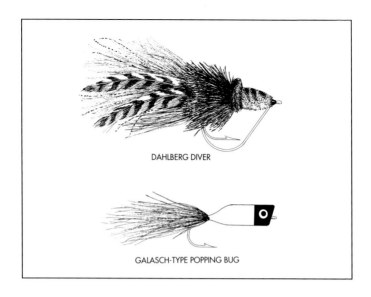

DAHLBERG DIVER

GALASCH-TYPE POPPING BUG

Peacock Bass Flies

as rock gardens. This is a section of river where huge boulders jut up from the bottom. Many times these rocks are as huge as a house, and contain broad ledges that interrupt the river's flow. The eddies and deep, slow-moving pockets of water that are created around these ledges are an ideal habitat for the larger peacock bass. They will hold close against such ledges and rocks, just as small-mouths do, and should be fished with standard small-mouth techniques.

Blind casting for peacocks along the shoreline is always exciting, especially if the water is a little roiled, for you never know when you'll get a smashing strike, and so you stay on your toes! The method here is to either throw a Deceiver, a Dahlberg Diver or a popping bug along the shoreline, working any area harder that looks like good bass habitat (grassbeds, rocks or ledges or any wood). You really don't have to be too far away, even as close as 40 feet or so, unless the water is very clear. But obviously, a longer retrieve will likely result in extra strikes.

My very favorite place to fish the pavons, especially the big peacock pavons, is in low clear water. The jungle rivers during the rainy season often get very high, flooding for great distances from the banks that contain the river during the drier portions of the year. But after the rainy season, much of the lower ground near the river turns into huge shallow lakes (called lagoons in South America). Such areas are breeding grounds for smaller fish, which in turn attract the pavons.

Well into the dry season these lagoons hold air-clear water in which you can sight-fish for pavons, much as you would for bonefish. The guide moves the boat slowly and quietly along while everyone looks for cruising fish. Many times, despite their gaudy colors, the most visible thing you'll see is the light bluish tinting on the tail. These fish are as spooky as a cat in a dog pound and will flee from any suspicious disturbance or a bad cast. Fly fishing for pavon in these conditions demands long, accurate casts — at least 60 feet.

In most lagoon situations, a long Deceiver dressed on a #1/0 hook, which lands with a relatively gentle splash, will trigger a strike. A floating line and a minimum of a 10-foot leader (I prefer a 12-footer) are required to achieve good presentations.

In the deep lakes, the best technique is to fish weedless Deceivers tight against the timber with a full-sinking line, like a Teeny T-200 or T-300.

Similarly, for the royal pavons, who like to hang out in the faster currents of the water, a full-sinking line is ideal for fishing a Deceiver in the down-and-across-current presentations that must frequently be made.

I know that many people recommend heavy fly rods for this kind of fishing, but if you will use Lefty's Deceivers or Dahlberg Divers (tied as I explained with a #1/0 hook) and a good graphite rod — such as those being manufactured today, for example, by Orvis, Loomis, Scott or Sage (I use a Sage RPL-X 8, which handles a weight-forward floating 9-weight or a Teeny T-300 sinking line superbly) — that is all the rod you need. Light graphite rods like these permit you to cast all day long without becoming exhausted.

There is some trade-off here, I admit. If a really big peacock immediately takes you into heavy structure, an 8-weight (or even a 9-weight) rod is not going to have the heavy backbone of a 12-weight to muscle the fish out. But I'd much rather lose the occasional fish than have to flail around all day with a 12-weight!

And since even big peacock bass are not likely to run for a long distance (they fight very hard but close to you, with much head shaking and short surges), you don't need more than 100 yards of backing on your reel.

Before departing from peacock bass, I just have to tell you about two other jungle fish, the *payara* and the *morocoto*, which are found in many of the same watersheds as the peacock bass.

The payara is a fantastic-looking fish. There are two holes in the top of its head, so that when its mouth is closed, its two long, saber-like teeth project from the lower jaw all the way through these two holes.

Inside its mouth are a number of smaller but similarly fierce looking teeth. Viewing the open mouth of one of these incredible fish is like looking into the jaws of a dragon. Payara are usually found in rivers where there is some current. This fish often gets to 20 pounds, jumps like a tarpon and fights well.

Peacock Bass and Morocoto Flies. From left to right, top row: two examples of Clouser Deep Minnow for morocoto; middle row: Popping Bug and Dahlberg Diver for peacock bass; bottom row: Lefty's Deceiver, white/chartreuse, and Lefty's Deceiver, white grizzly/tan for peacock bass.

The paraya feeds primarily on baitfish. Therefore, flies to interest it must look like baitfish, and the Deceiver patterns I described above for fishing peacock bass will work just fine. But the longer the fly, the better.

Of course, with a fearsome mouthful of teeth, you will need a wire leader — one no longer than six inches is all that's required. A longer one will make it difficult to cast. If you use braided wire, something testing between 25 and 40 pounds is ideal. If you prefer solid stainless steel trolling wire, #4 to #6 is suggested. While many people attach the wire to the leader with snaps or swivels, the best connections are knots, which make the leader less visible to the fish. Braided leader wire can be joined to the mono leader by an Albright knot, and a Haywire Twist in the solid wire, joined with an Albright is recommended.

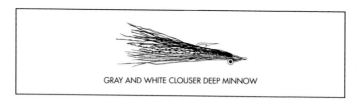

GRAY AND WHITE CLOUSER DEEP MINNOW

The morocoto is another fabulous fish often found in rivers where peacock bass exist. This is a tough battler. It is shaped somewhat like a bluegill, has a mouthful of sharp teeth and can weigh in excess of 20 pounds! Imagine what it would be like to hook up with a 20-pound bluegill and you'll have a good idea of how well this fish will strain your tackle!

The morocoto can often be found in long, slick glides in rivers, or near rocks where there is a current break. It feeds a great deal on small baitfish, two-to-four inches in length, and has a relatively small mouth, so large flies are useless. The best fly pattern I have found for them is a Clouser Deep Minnow no longer than your ring finger, in colors to imitate the local baitfish: a white belly and light brown or light gray top, with a bit of gold Flashabou or Crystal Flash in the wing, is a good choice. The same tackle used on peacocks works well on payara or morocoto.

I know this book is about bass, but if you are ever fortunate enough to go to South America for peacocks, don't forget to inquire about the payara and the morocoto. Both are unforgettable fish on a fly rod.

NIUGINI AND SPOTTAILED BASS

Some years ago I was introduced to the strongest fish for its size that I ever hooked. I have written for many years that saltwater fish are always stronger than those that live in freshwater. And, I am here to admit that I was wrong — very, very wrong.

There is a fish called the *Niugini bass* (sometimes referred to simply as a *black bass*). Niugini is the local spelling of the large South Pacific island we know as New Guinea, so when I talk about this fantastic fish, I'm talking about a watery terror that lives in the freshwater rivers of New Guinea. It may also exist in other remote watersheds in the Pacific basin, but no one — at least no fisherman I have ever talked to — really knows.

This basslike fish is a member of the Lutjanus cyanoterus family of fish, and is related to the cubera snapper — a fish slightly redder in coloration and which also has a fierce reputation — that lives on the ocean reefs in the Caribbean, Central America, and parts of South America.

The black bass has a close relative that swims alongside it in the freshwaters of New Guinea, the *spottailed bass*. Both the Niugini black bass and the spottailed bass are mostly green, darker on top than the sides, with a pale white to cream-colored belly. Upon examination of the two species, the only difference a non-scientist like myself can observe between them is that the spottailed has a large circular black spot near the tail. Excepting the spot, I can't see any difference in the two fish — including how well they fight. Both are armed with a series of teeth that resemble the canine teeth of a big dog. You can usually figure one fly for each caught fish.

Until very recently, even scientists knew very little about the Niugini bass and spottailed bass. I am told that Australian biologists captured a specimen that was only a few inches long. They thought it was a species of baitfish. How wrong they were! So far as I know, there are perhaps no more than two dozen anglers who have caught a Niugini black bass on a fly rod. And, less than a half dozen fly fishermen have landed both the black and spottailed bass. I have been fortunate to land several spottailed bass and quite a few black bass — but I had to pay my dues to achieve this distinction!

Let me tell you about my first experience with the Niugini black bass. I was lucky enough to spend several weeks fishing with some of Australia's best light tackle fishermen when we were making a film on light tackle fishing in the outback of northern Australia and New Guinea. If you know fly fishermen from Australia, you are probably aware that they are great practical jokers. Realizing this, I listened and didn't believe their advice about how to fish for the Niugini black bass and its kissing cousin, the spottailed. "You have to use 40-pound-test leaders directly between the fly and the line, mate," they insisted, "and if the fly line had a stronger core, you could really use a heavier leader."

At our base camp hacked out of the jungles along the Kulu River, I listened to this stuff. I was sure that they were kidding, and knew that if I actually rigged up with such strong tackle these Aussies would be telling all their friends for years to come about the joke they played on the hotshot Yank fisherman. Yet, on our first night in camp, I watched in considerable disbelief as they put together stout level-line casting rods with reels loaded with 40 and 50-pound-test monofilament. They even discarded their standard treble hooks and replaced them with extra-strong ones.

For their fly rods, they were rigging 40-pound-test leaders and attaching #3/0 to #5/0 stainless steel hooks dressed with huge six to eight-inch fly patterns similar to Dahlberg Divers and Half & Halfs, equipped with stout wire weedguards and 1/8 or 1/10-ounce lead eyes that would force these huge flies to sink deep and fast.

Still suspecting a trick, I rigged my two fly lines with 20-pound-test leaders — much heavier leaders than I normally ever use.

With my two Australian companions, the next morning we motored downriver. A trip down a New Guinea jungle river is a fantastic experience. The area appears untouched by man, and must look just the way it did when the first European explorers arrived several hundred years ago. You see natives paddling dugout canoes and hunting with bow and arrows. There are all sorts of exotic birds either sitting in the trees or flying overhead. There are huge hornbills, flocks of green and red parrots, and a dozen other kinds of birds. Crocodiles would leap into the river from mud bars where they had been enjoying the warm sun. Butterflies, some with a wingspan of six inches or more, fluttered through the air.

Running the boat was Dean Butler, who in my judgment is one of the finest young, all-around light tackle anglers in the world. Dean has superior fishing skills with fly, plug, spinning or offshore gear. My other companion was Rod Harrison, Australia's leading outdoor writer and fly fisherman supreme, who has battled just about every small and large fish that exists in his part of the world on both light tackle and fly rods. Incidentally, it was Rod who about 10 years ago began exploring New Guinea and began to write about these great fish — he calls them "river Rambos" — which he claimed were the strongest fish in the world but which nobody knew about until he brought some frozen specimens back.

I was in very good company indeed!

When I looked around the boat, I saw only my companions' two heavy casting outfits, armed with huge plugs; and their fly rods rigged with those extraordinary 40-pound-test leaders and huge flies. There was no other tackle in the boat, and I began to wonder if they really had been playing a joke on me!

As we moved downriver, Dean and Rod explained that a black bass will hide among the sunken branches of trees that have fallen into the jungle rivers. When an unwary prey swims by, the fish darts out, grabs it and then immediately returns to the safety of the tree branches. The fishing technique for them, then, is to locate a sunken tree along the shoreline, ease the boat within casting distance, throw the lure or fly to the edge of the branches, and begin a retrieve. Once the fish is hooked, the problem is to prevent it from swimming back to the safety of the submerged tree branches.

We got into position near the first tree and Dean put the boat into neutral. Rod said, "Have a go at it, Lefty." Still not sure that they weren't playing a trick on me, I insisted on Rod fishing first, while I watched. Dean sat in the rear of the boat with his hand on the outboard motor's shift lever, with the motor idling in neutral.

Rod picked up his casting rod — loaded, remember with 40-pound monofilament to which he had added a bite tippet of about a foot of 80-pound monofilament. Reaching into the holster on his side, he withdrew his pliers and proceeded to tighten the star drag on his reel. My eyes flew open. Bracing himself at the front of the boat, Rod threw the big plug well back among the limbs of the sunken tree and began his retrieve. Suddenly, a huge green shape appeared and grabbed the plug. Rod swept back on the rod with all his might. "Hit it Dean!" he yelled. Dean put the motor into reverse and while Rod struggled to hold the rod, the motor slowly began backing the boat and pulling the fish away from the tree. Suddenly, there was a sound like a rifle shot, and Rod staggered back in the boat. The 40-pound line had broken!

You can't believe how quickly I cut off my 20-pound leader and replaced it with one of 40-pound strength. Now armed with the heaviest leader I have ever used in fly fishing, tied to a 13-weight sinking line rigged onto a 12-weight rod (a casting rig I had previously used only on giant tarpon and sailfish), I cast under the branches of an overhanging tree. A large green shape appeared and I set the hook. "Hit it Dean!" I yelled, grabbing the line as tightly as I could. But to no avail. As the boat began to move backwards the fish dove for the submerged roots of the tree. That fish pulled so hard that the thick fly line sped through my clenched fist. In seconds the fish had tangled the line in the roots and had straightened my #3/0 stainless steel hook! I looked at my hand and there was a white stripe across my palm where the dry fly line had created a friction burn. No fish had ever treated me so roughly.

"Now you know why I named them river Rambos," Rod said.

From then on, since I found it impossible to hold the fly line after a large black or spottailed bass had taken my offering, I finally hit upon a way to stop these awesome fish from getting into the trees after the strike. After setting the hook hard, I immediately made two turns around my reel with the fly line. This is the only way I found to prevent them from taking line. The boat was then put into reverse and I held on until we could tow the critter out to open water where a normal fish-fight could take place. The first Niugini black bass I landed was an 18 pounder. My best to date is only about 25 to 28 pounds.

Several people have asked me how big black and spot-tailed bass can get. My answer is that speaking from my personal fishing experiences, I don't know — because the big ones I have hooked into have either straightened my

#3/0 to #5/0 hooks or have broken my 40-pound-test leaders!

But I have been witness to several incidents that show that the fish obviously do get very large indeed. Once, when one of my Australian friends hooked a Niugini bass of about 13 or 14 pounds, another monster bass rose out of the water and *swallowed* the other fish, *whole*, breaking the line easily.

On another occasion, Bob Marriott, a friend of mine who runs perhaps the largest fly shop in the world in Fullerton, California, was fighting a black bass of perhaps six to eight pounds. Using a powerful 10-weight saltwater rod, he had managed to lever the fish near the surface when suddenly a huge bass appeared, inhaled his hooked fish, and took off. Until Bob could get the line wrapped around the reel, it burned a white path across his hand. Then there ensued a brief tug-of-war, which finally ended when his line went limp. "I guess it broke the leader, Lefty. Did you see how big it was?" Bob asked as he reeled in. But the fish hadn't broken the leader. The smaller fish had been hooked in the bony portion of its lower jaw by a fly dressed on a heavy stainless steel #3/0 hook. The larger fish had simply pulled so hard on the smaller one it had swallowed, that it had actually straightened that heavy steel #3/0 hook!

Here are my tackle recommendations for fly fishing to Niugini black bass and spottailed bass.

Fly Rods — For the fly fisherman who is willing to accept the likely risk of losing a good deal of his terminal tackle, the lightest rod should be a 10-weight graphite designed for heavy saltwater fly fishing. A 12-weight graphite is the preferred size.

Fly Lines — Uniform-sinking or Teeny T-300 or T-400 lines are ideal for these underwater presentations. Of course, for Dahlberg Diver presentations, you need a weight-forward floating line.

Flies — All flies, surface or underwater, should carry heavy weedguards. If you need to fish either among sunken logs or around drowned trees, heavy weedguards are essential for protecting your flies.

The flies of choice are the Dahlberg Diver, for surface work, dressed on a strong #3/0 hook, with a large head and a total length of at least five inches (this is an excellent pattern for patrolling around the branches of a sunken tree), the Half & Half, again dressed on a heavy #3/0 or #4/0 hook with lead eyes of 1/8 to 1/10-ounce, the Lefty's Deceiver dressed also with heavy lead eyes and in darker colors. I also find it helpful to modify the pattern by using

Niugini and Spottailed Bass Flies. From left to right, top row: *Dahlberg Diver and Lefty's Deceiver with weedguard;* middle row: *Bend Back Fly;* bottom row: *Half & Half and Lefty's Deceiver dressed with a big eye.*

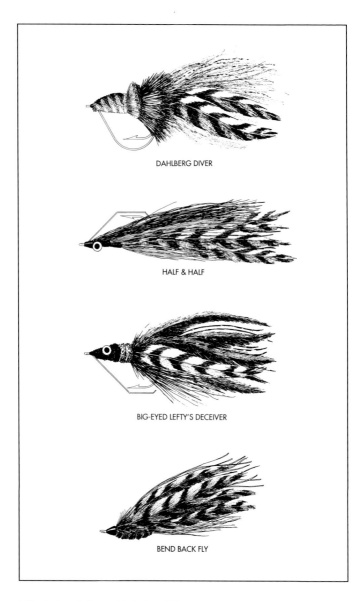

DAHLBERG DIVER

HALF & HALF

BIG-EYED LEFTY'S DECEIVER

BEND BACK FLY

Niugini and Spottailed Bass Flies

chenille, wrapped the length of the hook, to give it bulk; and a Bend Back Fly with the rear portion of the hook weighted with .030 lead wire. Darker colors seem to draw more strikes.

In more than 40 years of writing about the outdoors and fly fishing, and traveling all over the world, I have been fortunate enough to have caught most of the major species a fly fisherman would ever desire, including billfish, many offshore and inshore species, and almost every major freshwater fish. I'm here to tell you that the Niugini and spottailed bass are the strongest fish I have ever hooked on a fly line — and they live in freshwater! I hope that someday you will have the opportunity to fly fish for them.

INDEX

Adams, Les 123-124

Alabama 18

Arjjim Islands 23

Bartlett, Norm 52

"Bass-bug action" in rods 34

Branham, Joe 66

A BRIEF NATURAL HISTORY OF THE MAJOR SPECIES OF BASS 13-23

Brooks, Joe 51

Butler, Dean 133-134

Butterfly pavon *see* Peacock bass

California 17, 19, 59

Canada 15, 18, 19, 75, 91

Casting 11

Central America 8

Chesapeake Bay 51

Clouser, Bob 46

Columbia River (northwestern U.S.) 15

Crystal Flash 48, 60, 61, 63, 64, 108, 124, 125, 130

Dave's Bug Floatant 58

Delaware River (New York) 75

Depth finder 111

THE DIFFERENCES BETWEEN SMALL AND LARGEMOUTH BASS FROM AN ANGLER'S PERSPECTIVE 25-31

THE EXOTICS 121-139

Eyes (for flies) 42, 44, 45, 47, 48, 64-66, 108, 132, 137

Farm ponds 94-97

Flashabou 48, 60, 63, 64, 108, 124, 125, 130

Flatfish plug 59

Flies, bass 41-71
  Bartlett's Gerbubble Bug 52, 53, 60, 96
  Basic Largemouth Popper 52, 53, 56, 60
  Bend Back 137, 138, 139
  Clouser Crayfish 41, 42, 43, 44, 45, 46, 113
  Clouser Crippled Minnow 48
  Clouser Deep Minnow 42, 43, 44, 45, 46, 47, 49, 50, 61, 64, 66, 102, 104, 108, 109, 110, 111, 112, 114, 129, 130
  Dahlberg Diver 57, 58, 60, 112, 125, 126, 128, 129, 132, 136, 137, 138
  Dave's Hare Jig 60, 61, 62, 109, 110, 111
  Deer-Hair Bug 56, 57, 58, 60
  Gerbubble Bug 50, 51, 53, 60
  Gerbubble Bug (Whitlock style) 51
  Gold Ribbed Hare's Ear 42
  Half & Half 45, 46, 47, 49, 50, 61, 66, 104, 108, 109, 110, 111, 132, 137, 138
  Homer Rhodes Tarpon 47

Improved Basic Largemouth Popper 55, 60
In-line spinner 45, 66-68, 108
Largemouth flies 49-62
Lefty's Bug 42, 43, 44, 45, 46, 47, 54, 56, 102
Lefty's Deceiver 36, 46, 59, 61, 62, 96, 124, 125, 126, 127, 128, 129, 137, 138
Muskrat 42
Nymphs 42, 43, 99
Pencil Popper 50, 51, 53, 60, 111
Pop Lips 60, 62, 96, 109, 110
Popping bug, Galasch-type 125, 126, 129
Red & White Hackle 36, 45, 47, 48, 49, 50, 61, 66, 96, 97, 102, 104, 109, 118
Red Squirrel Tail 42
Seaducer 48
Smallmouth flies 41-48
Soft hackle 42, 43, 49, 50, 61, 99
Some general observations about the selection of 62-71
Water Wiggle Bug 49, 57, 59, 60, 96, 109, 110, 111
Woolly Bugger 36, 42, 43, 44, 45, 46, 49, 50, 61, 99, 102, 104, 109, 110, 111, 114
Floating lines 35, 88, 102, 103, 117, 128, 137
  Bass-bug taper 36
  Double taper 35
  Full sinking 36, 103-104, 109, 123, 136
  Shooting head 35
  Sink tip 36, 37, 127

Weight forward 35, 36, 37, 128
Florida 15, 17, 59
FLY FISHING FOR BASS IN RIVERS, LAKES, SMALL STREAMS AND PONDS 73-119
Full-sinking line applications 38
Georgia 17
Great Lakes 15
Harrison, Rod 132-135
Hooks
  barbless 71
  sharpness of 71
In-line spinner 66-68, 108
Irian Jaya (New Guinea) 23
James River (Virginia) 19, 74
John Day River (Oregon) 75
Juniata River (New York) 74
Kansas 18
Knots
  Albright 129
  Haywire Twist 67, 129
  Nail 117
Kula River (Papua New Guinea) 132
Lake Ontario (Canada) 18
Lakes 91-93
Large rivers 74-88
  Structures in large rivers 76-84
    Grassbeds 15, 16, 39, 76, 83-84, 94, 104, 108, 110, 111, 118
    Rocks 76-79, 89-90, 91-94, 96, 102, 105, 109, 114, 126

Wood 17, 76, 79-82, 105, 110
Use of boats, motors and anchors on 84-88
 Anchors
  Drag 86-87
  Mule 85
 Boats
  Canoes 84, 86-87
  Jet boats 84
  Jon boats 84, 85
Leaders 37, 38, 39-41, 61-62, 88, 103, 117, 127, 129, 132, 133, 135, 136
 Formula for constructing 40
 Tapered 40
Lines 35-39
Loomis, G. (Company) 128
Loving, Tom 51
Maine 91
Manaka Lodge (Venezuela) 122, 123
Marriott, Bob 136
Maryland 9, 15, 18
Mexico 8, 15
Mini-eddies 108
Minnesota 18, 91, 114
Mississippi River Valley 15
Morocoto 128, 130
Mueller, Gene 122
Netcraft Fishing Tackle Co. 67
New Britain 23
New Guinea see Papua New Guinea
New River (Virginia) 74
Niagara River (New York) 75

Night fishing for smallmouths 116-119
Niugini bass 22-23, 130-139
 Flies for 137-139
 Fly lines for 136-137
 Fly rods for 136
Ohio River (midwestern U.S.) 18-19
Oklahoma 18
Orinoco River (Venezuela) 22, 122, 125
Orvis Services, Inc. 128
Papua New Guinea 23, 131, 133
Pavon, see Peacock bass
Payara 128-130
Peacock bass 21-22, 121-130
Peacock pavon see Peacock bass
Pennsylvania 11
Penobscot River (Maine) 75
Pig and Jig Lure 60
Popovics, Bob 62
Potomac River (Maryland) 11, 19, 74
Rapala plug 44, 48
Reels 34-35
Rods 33-34
Royal pavon see Peacock bass
Sage 128
Scott Fly Rods 128
The seasons of the bass 98-113
 Cold weather 104-113
  Fishing lakes in 109-113
  Fishing large rivers in 105-109
 Late spring/early fall 103-104
 Summer 98-102

Shenandoah River (Virginia) 19, 74

Shooting head applications 38-39

Sink-tip line applications 36-38

Small streams 88-90

Snake River (Idaho) 75

South Carolina 17

Special techniques for retrieving bass 113-116

Spottailed bass *see* Niugini bass

St. Croix River (Minnesota) 75

Stripping guide
   Diameter of 34

Susquehanna River (Pennsylvania) 19, 74

TACKLE FOR BASS 33-71

Tank, Texas 114

Teeny Nymph lines 68, 109, 127, 128, 136-137

Testor's PLA hobby paints 64

Texas 59

Treasure Lake (Cuba) 8

Tullis, Larry 59

Ultra Hair 46, 124

Umpqua Feather Merchants 60-61

Ventuari River (Venezuela) 122, 125

Virginia 11, 18

Washington Times 122

Waterman, Charley 115

Watersheds for bass 74-97

Water temperature 26-31

Weedguards 45, 49, 51, 61, 68-71, 80, 94, 104, 111, 118, 123, 127, 132, 137

Weedless flies *see* Weedguards

West Irian *see* Irian Jaya (New Guinea)

White Miller mayfly hatch 100-102

Whitlock, Dave 51, 60, 116

Wind, importance of, to lake fisherman 112-113

FLY FISHING FOR BASS
SMALLMOUTH, LARGEMOUTH, EXOTICS